DK EYEWITNESS TRAVEL

TOP 10
ICELAND

D0433059

N

Penguin
Random
House

Top 10 Iceland Highlights

The Top 10 of Everything

CONTENTS

Iceland Area by Area

Streetsmart

Within each Top 10 list in this book, no hierarchy of quality or popularity is implied. All 10 are, in the editor's opinion, of roughly equal merit.

Front cover and spine *Reykjavík and Mount Esja in the background*
Back cover *Godafoss Falls, North Iceland*
Title page *Hveravellir hot spring in the western highlands*

Welcome to
Iceland

Land of the Vikings and their sagas. A mix of lunar deserts, thundering waterfalls, erupting volcanoes and majestic fjords. Hiking hotspot. Wildfowl mecca. All this only begins to describe Iceland... so who could deny it's Europe's wildest, most rugged destination? With Eyewitness Top 10 Iceland, it's yours to explore.

We love nothing more than spending never-ending summer days strolling **Reykjavík**'s historic centre, taking an outdoor thermal soak in the surreal waters of the **Blue Lagoon**, enjoying fresh-caught salmon or lobster in a seafront restaurant, tackling the **Laugavegur** trail between **Landmannalaugar**'s hot springs and the beautiful highland wilderness at Þórsmörk, or gazing at powder-blue icebergs drifting lazily around at **Jökulsárlón**. It's all here on this island nation, floating just below the Arctic Circle.

The country isn't all a struggle against the elements. Small but sophisticated Reykjavík offers a melange of cafés, bars and museums. History and landscape are visibly entangled at sites such as **Þingvellir**, the rift-valley location of Iceland's original Viking parliament, or **Laxárdalur**, the setting for the tragic *Laxdæla Saga*. But in the end, it's Iceland's raw beauty that really captures the imagination: the smouldering lava fields, huge volcanic craters, bubbling mud pools and seething geysers.

Whether you're coming for a weekend or a week, our Top 10 guide is designed to bring together the best of everything the country can offer, from four-wheel-drive expeditions across the Interior to gentle walks around Reykjavík's city parks. The guide gives you tips throughout, from seeking out when and where to see the **northern lights** to the best places to spot puffins, plus easy-to-follow itineraries, designed to tie together a clutch of sights in a short space of time. Add inspiring photography and detailed maps, and you've got the essential pocket-sized travel companion. **Enjoy the book, and enjoy Iceland**.

Clockwise from top: Jökulsárlón icebergs, the Blue Lagoon, Perlan building in Reykjavík, Eyjafjallajökull volcano erupting, Vík church, a puffin, turf houses in Djúpivogur

Exploring Iceland

Iceland's attractions are split between its unique island culture and its often explosive scenery – and with many landscapes closely tied to famous historic events, you'll often find both together. Here are some ideas for making the most of your stay, whether you are here on a weekend break in Reykjavík, or have time to circuit the country.

Reykjavík's old houses are weatherproofed in brightly coloured corrugated iron.

Strokkur geyser erupts every few minutes.

Þingvellir · Geysir · Gullfoss
Reykjavík
Kerið
Blue Lagoon · Selfoss
Hvolsvöllur Saga Centre · Eyjafjallajö
Seljalandsfoss
Skógafoss

Key
— Two-day itinerary
— Seven-day itinerary

Two Days in Iceland

Day ❶
Stroll around **Reykjavík**'s midtown and harbour *(see p75)*, taking in the **Harpa** theatre *(see p76)* and cultural exhibitions at **Landnámssýningin**, **Safnahúsið** and **Listasafn Íslands** *(see p75)*. In the afternoon, survey the city from atop **Hallgrímskirkja** *(see p76)* or **Perlan** *(see p77)* before admiring Modernist canvases at **Kjarvalsstaðir** *(see p76)*. Finish with the zoo and botanic gardens at **Laugardalur** *(see p77)*.

Day ❷
Take a Golden Circle tour (or drive) around the ancient parliament site at **Þingvellir** *(see pp12–13)*, **Geysir**'s hot pools and waterspouts *(see pp16–17)*

and the thundering falls of **Gullfoss** *(see pp18–19)*. Enjoy an evening soak at the **Blue Lagoon** *(see pp14–15)*.

Seven Days in Iceland

Day ❶
Explore **Reykjavík**'s historic midtown and harbour *(see p75)*, taking in the excellent, subterranean **Landnámssýningin** exhibition *(see p75)*. Drive around the iconic landscapes at **Þingvellir** *(see pp12–13)*, **Geysir** *(see pp16–17)* and **Gullfoss** *(see pp18–19)*, before heading past **Kerið** crater *(see p112)* to spend the night in the town of Selfoss.

Day ❷
Travel the southwest coast, via the **Hvolsvöllur Saga Centre** *(see p112)*,

0 kilometres 60
0 miles 60

Jökulsárlón lagoon is filled with floating blue icebergs.

Seljalandsfoss waterfall is fed by meltwater from Eyjafjallajökull icecap.

the waterfall at **Seljalandsfoss** *(see p44)*, the **Eyjafjallajökull** icecap *(see p46)* – site of the 2010 eruption – and **Skógafoss** waterfall *(see p45)*. Stay overnight at **Vík** *(see p110)*, with its teeming seabird colonies.

Day ❸
Cross the gravel desert that lies east of Vík to **Skaftafell** *(see p25)*, where you can see glacier tongues and **Svartifoss** waterfall *(see p60)*. Continue to the icebergs at **Jökulsárlón** *(see pp32–3)* and lobster restaurants at **Höfn** *(see p103)*, with views of **Vatnajökull** icecap *(see p24)* along the way.

Day ❹
Travel up the east coast and then inland to **Egilsstaðir** *(see p101)*, where you could either circuit

Lögurinn lake or head to the picturesque East Fjords port of **Seyðisfjörður** *(see p102)*.

Day ❺
Drive towards Lake Mývatn, detouring to explore the **Krafla** eruption site *(see p21)* and **Námaskarð**'s mud pools *(see p21)*. Circuit **Lake Mývatn** *(see p20)* before unwinding at **Jarðböðin Nature Baths** *(see p21)*.

Day ❻
Head to the north coast for a whale-watching trip out of **Húsavík** *(book in advance; see p96)*, before driving to pleasant **Akureyri** *(see p96)*.

Day ❼
Return to Reykjavík and spend a couple of hours at the **Blue Lagoon** *(see pp14–15)* en route to the airport.

Top 10 Iceland Highlights

Jökulsárlón lagoon at sunset

🔟 Iceland Highlights

Iceland sits on an active volcanic ridge at the edge of the Arctic Circle. Only birds and foxes inhabited the land when Vikings arrived in the 8th century to found the commonwealth of the Saga Age. Towns were not established until the 18th century. Today, it has a hi-tech infrastructure and most of its 320,000 population lives around Reykjavík.

Þingvellir National Park **1**

This broad rift valley, where the tectonic plates are visibly tearing apart in a riot of geology was the site of Iceland's Viking parliament (pp12–13).

2 The Blue Lagoon

Take a sauna or soak in the pale blue waters of Iceland's most sublime outdoor spa set among black lava boulders (see pp14–15).

3 Geysir Hot Springs Area

Just an hour from Reykjavík, this hillside of bubbling pools and erupting waterspouts has given its name to similar formations around the world (see pp16–17).

Gullfoss **4**

This powerful waterfall has been a national symbol since it was saved from oblivion during the 1920s (see pp18–19).

5 Lake Mývatn Area

Lake Mývatn collects the best of Iceland in one place: wildfowl, volcano cones, mud pits, steaming lava flows and thermal pools (see pp20–21).

Ísafjörður
Gjögur
Þingeyri
Bíldudalur
Hólmavík
8 Látrabjarg Bird Cliffs
Brjánslækur
Laugar
Breiðafjörður
Ólafsvík
Stykkishólmur
Brú
7
Vegamót
Snæfellsjökull National Park
Bifröst
Borgarnes
Langjök
Faxaflói
Þingvellir National Park **1**
Gullfoss **4**
Reykjavík
Geysir Hot Springs Are **3**
The Blue Lagoon **2**
Selfoss
Hvolsvöllur

⑥ Vatnajökull National Park

This reserve protects not only the Vatnajökull icecap and its outrunning glaciers, but also beautiful rivers, gorges and mountain formations *(see pp24–5)*.

Snæfellsjökull National Park ⑦

Western Iceland's peninsula peaks with the snowy cone of Snæfellsjökull, a slumbering volcano crossed by hiking trails. It is tall enough to be visible from Reykjavík *(see pp26–7)*.

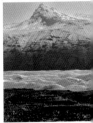

Látrabjarg Bird Cliffs ⑧

Fantastically remote even by Icelandic standards, north-westerly Látrabjarg supports one of the largest seabird colonies in Europe, and is home to millions of gulls, guillemots and puffins *(see pp28–9)*.

Map labels:
Kópasker
Siglufjörður
Þórshöfn
Dalvík
Bakkafjörður
Sauðárkrókur
Reykjahlíð
Grímsstaðir
Vopnafjörður
Akureyri
⑤ Lake Mývatn Area
Bakkagerði
Egilsstaðir
Eskifjörður
Hofsjökull
Djúpivogur
Vatnajökull
⑥ Vatnajökull National Park
Höfn
⑩ Jökulsárlón
⑨ Landmannalaugar Area
Skaftafell
Fagurhólsmýri
Kirkjubæjarklaustur

0 km 60
0 miles 60

Vík

⑩ Jökulsárlón

Make a tour along the Ringroad to this lagoon between the Breiðamerkurjökull glacier and the Atlantic Ocean, full of seals and icebergs *(see pp32–3)*.

⑨ Landmannalaugar Area

Its bridgeless rivers, shattered grey mountains and hot springs make you feel like an explorer in the wilds, but summer buses make this area easily accessible *(see pp30–31)*.

TOP 10 ⭐ Þingvellir National Park

Iceland's location on the mid-Atlantic ridge is obvious at Þingvellir (Assembly Plains), where the land has crashed in a deep scar stretching north from Lake Þingvallavatn. In AD 930, this dramatic setting was chosen by the island's 36 chieftains as the site of their annual Alþing (General Assembly). The country's entire population of 60,000 gathered to hear the laws and to settle disputes, occasionally by combat. The Alþing's power declined after Iceland accepted Norwegian sovereignty in 1262, but the assembly continued to be held here until 1798.

1 Lögberg (Law Rock)
A prominent outcrop below Almannagjá's cliffs marks the site where the Alþing's Lawspeaker stood and recited the country's laws to the masses below. Look nearby for faint outlines of *buðir*, the tented camps used during Viking times.

2 Þingvellir Church
This surprisingly low-key wooden building with a black roof **(below)** is a reminder of the Alþing of AD 1000, when, despite strong opposition from pagan priests, the Icelandic nation adopted Christianity as its sole religion under threat of Norwegian invasion *(see p36)*. The church was built in 1859 but it has a pulpit that dates back to 1683.

3 Volcanic Features
The broad, flattened dome of northerly Skjaldbreiður – an ancient shield volcano – was the source of the lava flow now covering Þingvellir's valley. Cut by deep fissures, the lava cooled into rough *a'a* outcrops and pavements of smoother *pahoehoe* (both of which are types of lava).

4 Almannagjá
A walk through Almannagjá's deep, cliff-lined gully **(above)** is a good way to appreciate Þingvellir's geology. Here, as the North American and European continental plates drift apart at a rate of 2.5 cm (1 inch) a year, Iceland is literally ripping in half.

5 Þingvallavatn
At 84 sq km (33 sq miles), Þingvallavatn **(below)** is the largest natural lake in Iceland. Its clear waters are famous for char and trout fishing, as well as scuba diving.

6 Flora
Þingvellir valley's floor is covered in a thick carpet of moss, lichen, orchids, dwarf willow and birch. Visit in autumn for exceptional colours and join the locals in picking crowberries **(left)**, used to make jam.

7 Visitor Centre
Perched atop the western side of the rift, on Route 36, the Visitor Centre offers superb views of Þingvellir. It also shows multilingual films and has a range of DVDs on the region's geology and history.

PAYING THE PENALTY

Law courts at the Alþing strangely had no power to enforce their judgments. Litigants accepted the verdicts because they reflected public opinion, but in theory – and sometimes in practice – powerful men could ignore sentences against them. The courts tried to resolve serious disputes through mediation, though the highest penalty in Viking times was not execution but being outlawed (banished from Iceland) for three years.

8 Wildlife
The area just to the north of Þingvallavatn's lakeshore abounds in interesting wildlife. Keep an eye out for swans, mergansers **(above)** and northern divers on the water, as well as snipes, ptarmigans, minks and Arctic foxes on land.

NEED TO KNOW

MAP C5 ■ From Reykjavík, Golden Circle tour buses visit Þingvellir daily year-round. Some 6 and 6a buses and summer services using the Kjölur route also stop here. If driving, allow 60–90 minutes via Route 36. ■ Bus schedule: www.bsi.is ■ www.thingvellir.is/english

■ From the Visitor Centre, through Almannagjá, descend to the Law Rock. Take a detour to see Peningagjá and the church, then walk up to Öxarárfoss. In good weather follow hiking tracks up the rift to some abandoned farms, but take care as the dense undergrowth hides deep fissures.

■ The only place to eat is the café at the Visitor Centre near Öxarárfoss.

9 Öxarárfoss
Legend has it that the falls were created when Öxará river **(right)** was diverted around AD 930 to provide drinking water during the assemblies. During medieval times, executions were also carried out here.

10 Peningagjá
Peningagjá is an extraordinary sight: a narrow but deep lava fissure flooded with clear, peacock-blue water. At the bottom of this naturally created wishing well you can see the glinting coins left by hopeful visitors.

🔟⭐ The Blue Lagoon and Around

The Blue Lagoon (*Bláa Lónið*) is Iceland's premier geothermal spa and one of the country's most beautiful. Set in a desolate lava wilderness, the lagoon's bright blue waters add a surreal splash of colour. You can laze in the steaming waters, have a beauty treatment, enjoy an excellent meal or stay nearby and catch the seasonal display of the aurora borealis. If you have your own transport, consider taking a detour to see some unusual sights: Grindavík's Saltfish Museum, the Seltún Hot Springs and Selatangar's abandoned fishing camp.

1 Background and Origin
The Blue Lagoon was created when superheated seawater flowing out of the Svartsengi Geothermal Power Station collected in the surrounding lava **(above)**. Locals discovered that a warm dip cured skin ailments and public facilities opened here during the 1980s.

2 Unique Lava Setting
The lagoon is bordered by rough masses of black lava boulders, which lie piled high around the perimeter, hemming in the powder-blue waters.

3 Geothermal Spa
The water, at a temperature of 37°C (99°F), is comfortable and the huge pool **(below)** is an amazing place to unwind, with an adjacent sauna.

4 Spa Services
Enjoy a relaxing massage in a private area of the lagoon itself **(above)**, or opt for a cleansing rub-down using the naturally processed fine silica, minerals, algae and salt distilled from the Blue Lagoon's waters. Beauty treatments are also available. It is a good idea to book any spa treatments in advance.

5 Dermatology and Health Clinics
The Blue Lagoon's mineral salts and white clay have long enjoyed a reputation for quickly curing eczema, psoriasis and other skin problems. You can seek specialized treatment while staying at the clinic near the lagoon or simply buy preparations that you can use at home.

6 LAVA Restaurant

Enjoy Icelandic dishes, such as grilled lobster with garlic butter or fillet of lamb, with a view of the lagoon from your table. There's also an excellent bar accessible from the water and a café selling snacks.

7 Icelandic Saltfish Museum

At Grindavík, a short drive south, is this eccentric museum (left) that traces the fishing heritage of Iceland through dioramas and photographs.

GEOTHERMAL POWER

Svartsengi Geothermal Power Station takes advantage of its location over a fault line to provide cheap, green power and heating for Reykjavík. Seawater is pumped over 1 km (0.6 miles) underground, turns to steam and is used to drive the turbines that help produce 76 MW of electricity. The steam is then cooled and released into the Blue Lagoon. Five geothermal plants produce a quarter of the nation's electricity.

8 Overnight Stay

Options for over-night accommodation include the Blue Lagoon Clinic and the Northern Lights Inn – the latter is a particularly fantastic spot during the winter, when the colourful aurora borealis can at times be seen playing across the night sky.

9 Seltún Hot Springs

About 22 km (13 miles) east of the lagoon are the Seltún Hot Springs (below). One of the geysers exploded in 1999. Walk the boardwalk to explore the steaming vents.

10 Selatangar

This village 15 km (9 miles) from the lagoon was abandoned in the 1850s. Ruins are visible through black sand dunes and lava outcrops.

NEED TO KNOW

MAP B5 ■ The Blue Lagoon, 240 Grindavík ■ Several tour buses daily from Reykjavík's BSÍ station. Bus information: www.re.is ■ 420 8800 ■ www.bluelagoon.com

Open Jan–May: 10am–8pm; Jun–Aug: 8am–10pm; Sep–Dec: 10am–8pm ■ Adm: ISK5,200–24,500 (pre-booking essential)

Icelandic Saltfish Museum: **MAP B5**
Seltún Hot Springs: **MAP B5**
Selatangar: **MAP B5**

■ The Blue Lagoon's high mineral content can damage your hair – protect it by rubbing in conditioner before a swim and make sure you shampoo thoroughly afterwards.

■ Apart from the main restaurant, there is a basic café at the Blue Lagoon's entrance where you can buy coffee, cold drinks and snacks.

🔟 ⭐ Geysir Hot Springs Area

The Geysir Hot Springs area lies on the lower slopes of Bjarnarfell, 90 minutes northeast of Reykjavík, and comprises a dozen or more hot water blowholes, including Geysir, the spout that gave its name to other geysers worldwide. The area became active about 1,000 years ago and today the most impressive spout is Strokkur, which you will definitely see in action. Geysir's pool is far larger but count yourself lucky if you see more than bubbles. Visit Haukadalur for an interesting old church and some undemanding hiking.

① **Geysir Hot Spring**
Geysir, "the Gusher" **(above)**, has not erupted to its full 70-m (230-ft) height since the mid-20th century, though until it was banned in the 1980s, dumping soap powder into the pool used to trigger a hiccup or two.

② **Blesi**
Up the slope behind the Geysir area, Blesi, "the Blazer", is a set of twin pools, one clear and scalding; the other cooler, opaque and powder blue with dissolved minerals **(below)**.

③ **Konungshver**
Catch the "King's Spring" on a sunny day and the colours are stunning. The clear, vivid blue water sits in a depression of orange-red rock. Get views from here of the rest of the Geysir area.

④ **Strokkur**
Strokkur, "the Churn" **(above)**, reliably erupts every few minutes, its clear blue pool exploding in a 15–30 m- (50–100 ft-) high spout with little noise. In between eruptions, watch the water sighing and sinking as the pressure builds.

⑤ **Litli Geysir**
Often overlooked on the way to Strokkur, Litli Geysir **(below)** is off the path to the left. It was likely once a waterspout that blew itself apart, and is now a violently slushing muddy pool, belching steam and bubbles.

6 **Hótel Geysir**
Guests at this hotel **(above)**, across the road from the famous Geysir hot spring, can enjoy the geothermal water at its indoor spa. A lunch buffet and evening menu are on offer at the restaurant.

7 **Haukadalur Church**
In a woodland about 2 km (1 mile) behind Geysir, this church has a ring on the door said to have been given to a local farmer by a giant, Bergþór, whose burial mound lies nearby.

THERE SHE BLOWS!
Geysers are formed in deep, vertical, flooded vents known as pipes. The water at the bottom of the pipe comes into contact with hot rock and boils, expanding upwards, while the cooler water at the surface of the geyser forms a kind of lid, trapping the rising water, until so much pressure builds up that the geyser explodes skywards. Watch Strokkur and you can clearly see this lid of cooler water bulging upwards just before each eruption.

8 **Haukadalur Forest**
Since the 1940s, Iceland's forestry service has planted millions of larches, pine and rowan trees in the Haukadalur valley. An easy walking trail through the area passes through a gully full of waterfalls.

NEED TO KNOW

MAP C5 ▪ The Geysir area is right by the roadside on Route 35, about 90 min from Reykjavík. ▪ Tour buses are available from Reykjavík's BSÍ station. Bus schedule: www.bsi.is

Hótel Geysir: www.geysircenter.com

▪ Stay on boardwalks or marked trails and do not step into pools or their outflows, as the water is boiling hot. Falling spray from Strokkur is cool, but you will need a raincoat if you are standing downwind.

▪ The Geysir Centre has a café that serves coffee, hot dogs, drinks and sandwiches, but the hotel restaurant, although it is pricier, actually offers better value for money.

Geysir Centre **9**
Directly across the road from the hot springs, the Geysir Centre has a souvenir shop **(right)**, a café and an entertaining exhibition on the history and geology of geysers. Do not miss a ride on the Earthquake Simulator.

10 **Bjarnarfell**
It takes a steep hike to reach the 727 m (2,385 ft) summit of Bjarnarfell, the hill overlooking Geysir, but the rewards on a good day are spectacular views of the red-brown rock and green fields surrounding the springs.

TOP 10 ⭐ Gullfoss

The powerful two-tier waterfalls at Gullfoss on the Hvítá river present a stunning sight, whether part-frozen in winter, in full flood during the spring melt, or roaring away during the long summer twilight. Their setting in a deep canyon adds to the spectacle, as does the landscape of icy peaks and gravel desert immediately north – quite a contrast to the green, spray-fed vegetation closer to the river. Take care at Gullfoss and always supervise children, as paths are slippery and there are no safety railings or warning signs.

1 Origin of Names
The clouds of rainbow-tinged spray hanging over it gave Gullfoss its name – the Golden Falls. Hvítá (White River) is named after the light-coloured glacial sediment it carries.

2 Geology
 The area's volcanic history can be seen on the cliffs opposite the viewing platform, with their distinct banded ash layers from separate volcanic eruptions, overlaid with basalt **(above)**.

3 The Canyon
The canyon continues downstream from Gullfoss for 2 km (1 mile), through basalt columns **(below)**. You can follow the track along the top or take a white-water rafting trip.

5 View from the Top
The main viewing area, and the safest, is the platform on the top of the canyon **(above)**. Orient yourself and take in the dramatic setting.

View from Below 4
 Soaked by the spray, you can really appreciate the sheer scale of the waterfalls from this vantage point: the river drops 10 m (33 ft), turns a right angle and then drops again **(right)**.

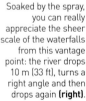

⑥ Plaque for Sigríður Tómasdóttir

A commemorative plaque to Sigríður Tómasdóttir **(left)** recalls her successful campaign to save these waterfalls from being drowned by a dam project.

⑦ Sigríðarstofa

The local exhibition centre, Sigríðarstofa, showcases the hardships of traditional life in the area, which is caught between relatively fertile plains to the west and the sterile wilderness of Iceland's frozen Interior directly north.

SAVING GULLFOSS

In 1907, landowner Einar Benediktsson signed away Gullfoss to be submerged by the construction of a hydroelectric dam across the Hvítá river. Sigríður Tómasdóttir, whose father was involved in the deal, was so incensed that she took legal action against the developers. Although she lost the case, public opinion ran so high in her favour that construction never began and Gullfoss was later donated to the nation of Iceland as a special reserve.

⑧ Visitor Centre

The roomy cafeteria at the Gullfoss Visitor Centre serves a delicious lamb soup. The falls are invisible from here but the views show mountains and glaciers.

⑨ Souvenir Shop

The gift shop at the Visitor Centre sells nothing specific to Gullfoss apart from postcards, but it is still a good place to find T-shirts, designer outdoor gear, books on Iceland and lava jewellery.

NEED TO KNOW

MAP D4 ■ Daily tour buses from Reykjavík's BSÍ station. www.bsi.is

■ Visit in winter when Gullfoss is partly frozen and hidden behind spectacular ice curtains; in summer, the afternoon provides the best lighting conditions for photographs.

■ Make sure you try the traditional lamb soup at the Visitor Centre café – and the refills are free.

⑩ Kjölur

This 160-km- (100-mile-) long route **(above)**, runs north from here across the Interior, traversing the gravel plains between the Langjökull and Hofsjökull icecaps.

TOP 10 ⭐ Lake Mývatn Area

Known as Midge Lake in English, Mývatn is a peaceful spread of water east of Akureyri and home to flocks of wildfowl in summer. The surrounding landscape, however, is anything but tranquil, with Mývatn hemmed in by a spectacular mix of extinct cinder cones and twisted lava formations, hot bathing pools, boiling mud pits and screaming volcanic vents. North-shore Reykjahlíð is Mývatn's main settlement, where you can organize tours to local sights and also to the Askja caldera in the barren Interior.

① Lake Mývatn
Spring-fed and covering 36 sq km (14 sq miles), Lake Mývatn was created during volcanic activity about 4,000 years ago. Lava formations **(above)** dominate the northern and eastern sides of the lake, while the rest of the shoreline is marshy.

③ Dimmuborgir
This weird, tumbled mass of indescribably contorted lava formations makes for an eerie hour-long wander on marked paths. Make sure you visit the drained lava tube known as Kirkja ("the Church") and keep your eyes open for the rare and endangered gyrfalcons.

④ Waterfowl Crossroads
Insect larvae and algae in Mývatn's shallow waters provide abundant food for phalaropes, swans, divers, Slavonian grebes and 13 species of duck, including the rare Barrow's goldeneye **(below)**, which breeds in the lake from May to August.

② Pseudocraters
Looking like bonsai volcanoes, pseudocraters **(above)** were formed by steam blisters popping through hot lava as it flowed over marshland. There are plenty of pseudocraters around Mývatn but the best, covered in walking tracks, are at Skútustaðir.

⑤ Jarðböðin Nature Baths

Like the Blue Lagoon *(see pp14–15)*, Jarðböðin **(above)** offers the chance to steam in the open-air, mineral-rich geothermal waters. The views here – of the lake and volcanic setting – are even better.

⑦ Laxá

Laxá, or the Salmon River, drains out of Lake Mývatn and then runs to the sea near Húsavík. Walk along its banks to see harlequin ducks tumbling in the rough waters between May and July.

KRAFLA FIRES

Earthquakes between 1975 and 1984 opened up a long volcanic fissure at Leirhnjúkur, just west of Krafla volcano, an event that became known as the Krafla Fires. Lava poured out over the plain here, leaving behind a fascinating expanse of still-smoking formations that you can reach and explore on foot from Krafla. It is not an excursion for the faint-hearted, however, as the paths are rough and you need to be careful to avoid some dangerously hot spots.

⑧ Krafla

Located northeast of Mývatn, Krafla volcano last erupted during the 1720s, when its lava nearly consumed Reykjahlíð's church. Víti, Krafla's flooded crater, is bright blue **(left)**.

⑥ Hverfjall

 This 400-m- (1,312-ft-) high cinder cone is made up of volcanic ash and gravel. There are fantastic views from the well-marked path around the crater's rim.

⑨ Askja

To the south of Mývatn is Askja, an 8-km- (5-mile-) wide flooded caldera. The Víti crater nearby exploded in 1875, causing a virtual exodus of the northeast.

NEED TO KNOW

MAP F2 ■ There are local buses and tours from Akureyri. There is also an airstrip at Reykjahlíð.

■ In summer you will need to buy face netting from local stores to protect yourself from irritating – though mostly harmless – swarms of tiny flies. They are worse on windless days.

■ The Gamli Bærinn bistro-bar at Reykjahlíð has good coffee, light meals, *hverabrauð* (ryebread baked in geothermal pits) and smoked trout from the lake.

⑩ Námaskarð

Among a landscape of red clay with yellow and white streaks, Námaskarð is an area of violently bubbling, sulphurous mud pits **(below)**. Take great care as you explore.

Following pages Dettifoss waterfall cascading into the Jökulsárgljúfur canyon

TOP 10 ⭐ Vatnajökull National Park

Vatnajökull National Park covers around 13,920 sq km (5,375 sq miles), 14 per cent of Iceland's surface, and comprises the Vatnajökull icecap and disconnected areas around its fringes. The long canyons and enormous waterfalls at Jökulsárgljúfur, Skaftafell's high moorland and paired glaciers, Lónsöræfi's wilderness and the remains of Lakagígar's catastrophic volcanic event can keep you occupied for days. Hiking, ice-climbing, snowmobiling and even dog-sledding are among the activities possible within this huge park.

1 Vatnajökull

Europe's largest icecap, Vatnajökull dominates the views inland from the southwest. A dozen or more glaciers slide inexorably coastwards off its top **(below)**. At least one active volcano smoulders away underneath.

2 Glacial Features

Glaciers are slow-moving rivers of ice advancing just a few centimetres a year (though most of Iceland's are shrinking). Extreme pressure grinds down underlying rock to leave gravel moraine ridges and squeezes out the air, giving them their blue colour.

3 Birdlife

Sandar, or deep beaches of black sand washed out from beneath Iceland's glaciers, provide nesting grounds for the greater skua **(left)**, an aggressive brown seabird that preys on weaker birds and their young.

4 Hvannadalshnúkur

A *nunatak* (rocky peak) protruding from Vatnajökull's icecap at 2,110 m (6,923 ft), this is Iceland's highest point. You need considerable experience to climb it.

5 Ásbyrgi

This gorge **(above)** is said to be a hoof print left by the Norse god Óðin's eight-legged horse, Sleipnir. Geologists say floods under Vatnajökull carved it.

6 Lakagígar
This 25-km (16-mile) row of craters **(below)** was created by a terrible eruption in 1783. Lava and poisonous gas wiped out the farms in the Kirkjubæjarklaustur area, causing a nationwide famine.

7 Skaftafell
Do not miss Svartifoss **(left)**, a waterfall framed by hexagonal basalt columns, in this national park that extends over 1,700 sq km (657 sq miles) of accessible highland plateau. Other highlights of this park include close-ups of blue glacier tongues streaked in gravel and superlative hiking along marked trails.

FLASH FLOOD

Jökulhlaups (glacial flash floods) happen when geothermal heating from volcanoes under the icecaps melts enough water to form an enclosed lake. If the lake dam gives way, the water explodes outwards with devastating results. A single prehistoric *jökulhlaup* carved out the Jökulsárgljúfur canyon, while a smaller event in 1996 sent water rushing out from under the Vatnajökull icecap, sweeping away 7 km (5 miles) of the highway near Skaftafell.

8 Jökulsárgljúfur
The name of this national park means "Glacier River Canyon", a reference to the 120-m- (394-ft-) deep and 500-m- (1,640-ft-) wide slash through which flows Jökulsá, Iceland's second-longest river.

9 Lónsöræfi
This private reserve, stretching from coastal lagoons through fractured orange rhyolite mountains, can be accessed by hiking.

NEED TO KNOW

MAP F4 ■ Summer-only buses to Ásbyrgi and Dettifoss from Akureyri; to Skaftafell from Reykjavík and Höfn; to Lakagígar from Kirkjubæjarklaustur and Höfn. Lónsöræfi and Hvannadalshnúkur accessible only to experienced hikers. Tours to Vatnajökull by Jeep, dog-sled and snowmobile from Höfn. ■ www.vatnajokulsthjodgardur.is

■ Most sections of Vatnajökull National Park are completely inaccessible in winter, closed due to bad weather or lack of buses. Plan a trip between July and mid-August to have the greatest choice of places to visit.

■ There are few places to eat within the park, so make sure you stock up on refreshments from the nearest town.

10 Dettifoss
Said to be Europe's most powerful waterfall, Dettifoss **(below)** sits amidst a jagged grey basalt land-scape, its 45-m (148-ft) drop sending clouds of spray skywards. Summer-only access is along a gravel road.

TOP10 ⭐ Snæfellsjökull National Park

Established in 2001, Snæfellsjökull National Park protects the snowy snout of the Snæfellsnes Peninsula, which juts 70 km (44 miles) into the sea from the western coast. Just two hours drive from Reykjavik with a beautiful conical volcano at its core, Snæfellsjökull is a place steeped in ancient, literary and New Age folklore, though most people who visit today are more interested in the mountain's hiking or climbing potential. Snæfellsjökull also makes a splendid backdrop for delving into the area's fishing history or for bird-watching.

1 Snæfellsjökull
Snæfellsjökull is the 1,445-m-(4,745-ft-) high icecap covering the dormant volcano, which last erupted in AD 250. The white cone of the volcano **(below)** is clearly visible to the north of Reykjavík on a clear day, rising up above Faxaflói Bay.

2 Coastal Boundary
The rugged coast of the Snæfellsnes Peninsula acts as a barrier between the rougher weather to the north and the generally drier, sunnier south. Strong storms with snowfall on the higher ground may occur throughout the year.

3 Djúpalónssandur
A pretty pebble beach near Dritvík **(above)**, where four heavy stones – "Useless", "Half-Strength", "Puny" and "Full-Strength" – were once used to test the brawn of applicants for fishing boat crews.

4 Hellnar
Home town **(left)** of an Icelandic woman, Guðríður Þorbjarnardóttir, who travelled widely in the Middle Ages – as far as Greenland, Rome and America.

5 Dritvík
Some 24 km (15 miles) from Hellissandur, for centuries this bay harboured what was once the busiest fishing fleet in the area. It is a good place to take a break and reflect upon changing times.

6 Bird-Watching
Large white-tailed sea eagles **(above)** are often seen in the vicinity of Snæfellsjökull National Park, although these rare birds mainly inhabit the Westfjords. Apart from these, the coastline supports the usual seabirds and wildfowl.

9 Ascending Snæfellsjökull
Experienced hikers can spend a day climbing Snæfellsjökull and enjoy the view from the top. It is also possible to sled up and ski down the mountain. However, neither of these activities should be attempted without the assistance of a guide. Get advice from the Visitor Centre or the National Park office before starting the hike.

JOURNEY TO THE CENTRE OF THE EARTH

Snæfellsjökull sprang to fame in Jules Verne's novel *Journey to the Centre of the Earth,* in which a German professor and his nephew decode an ancient manuscript and use the instructions to descend into Snæfellsjökull's crater on a subterranean journey of exploration. Such craters were traditionally feared here as the literal entrances to hell, a belief that left many mountains unscaled till the 19th century.

10 Bárður's Statue
A terrific split stone statue of folk figure Bárður Snæfellsás stands near Arnarstapi. According to legend, Bárður was an early settler in the area and his protective spirit still lives on Snæfell and watches over the village.

7 Hiking the National Park
From Hellissandur, several circular hiking trails explore the lava fields and coastline west of Snæfellsjökull. Expect to encounter little beaches, rugged seascapes, rare plants, birdlife and seals.

8 Arnarstapi
Set at the foot of Snæfellsjökull's southeast corner, Arnarstapi **(below)** is a tiny fishing village, where a rocky arch known as Gatklettur stands out to sea. You can also organize snowcat trips onto Snæfellsjökull from here.

NEED TO KNOW

MAP A4 ▪ Snæfellsjökull National Park's main office: Klettsbúð 7, Hellissandur; 436 6860; www. snaefellsjokull.com; open summer: 10am–6pm; winter: noon–4pm ▪ Visitor Centre: Hellnar; 436 6888; open 10am–5pm daily ▪ Buses from Reykjavík to Hellissandur: www.bsi. is, www.straeto.is ▪ www.ust.is

▪ **To climb Snæfellsjökull you need ice axes, crampons and weatherproof gear. Talk to National Park officers at Hellissandur and Hellnar Visitor Centre about your route and the weather conditions.**

▪ **Hellissandur's Café Gamla Rif serves a tasty fish soup.**

🔟 ⭐ Látrabjarg Bird Cliffs

The Látrabjarg bird cliffs are just about as remote a place as you can readily reach in Iceland. Traditionally a farming area, the region has become almost depopulated since the 1960s, leaving Látrabjarg to the millions of seabirds that return here to breed during the summer months. Most people come here to see the abundant numbers of charismatic puffins. On the way there is also a worthwhile folk museum and an amazing beach at Breiðavík – probably the last thing you would expect to find in this part of the world.

1 Látrabjarg Cliffs

The 14-km- (9-mile-) long and 440-m- (1,444-ft-) high cliffs (**below**) form a colossal bird colony with millions of seabirds including puffins, cormorants, kittiwakes, razorbills and guillemots, nesting here every year.

2 Geology

Iceland's western extremity is home to its oldest geological formations. The layered cliffs are a slice through the past, each distinct band – clearly visible despite the birdlife – recording the different volcanic events.

3 Bird Apartments

Species nest at different heights, forming banded apartments: puffins at the top, then razorbills, fulmars and kittiwakes (**below**), with guillemots on the sheer cliff ledges.

4 Puffins

The most amiable residents of Látrabjarg are the puffins (**above**). These small seabirds have orange feet and multicoloured, sail-shaped bills. They nest in grassy burrows at the top of the cliffs and often tolerate being approached, but do be cautious.

5 Eggs

Due to their habit of favouring crowded, sheer cliffs as places for nesting, guillemot eggs are conical – a shape that protects the precious cargo contained within them by causing the shells to roll in a circular movement around their tip rather than rolling over the edge.

Guano
You cannot fail to notice the strong smell of guano, or dried bird droppings, in the air at Látrabjarg. The thick, spongy grass that grows at the top of the cliffs **(right)** exists thanks to centuries of fertile guano deposits. Without them, the puffins would not have anywhere to dig their nests.

Látrabjarg History 7
The Látrabjarg cliffs were, until 1926, a favourite summer haunt for local farmers, who would scale the cliffs to collect bird eggs. Puffins were once caught and eaten in large numbers, a practice that continues to this day in the southern islands of Vestmannaeyjar *(see p110).*

Bjargtangar 8
This westernmost point of Europe is marked by the lonely beacon of the Bjargtangar lighthouse **(right)**, a small, whitewashed and distinctly weatherbeaten building perched high up on the grassy clifftop. The light-house marks the beginning of the Látrabjarg cliffs. A warning sign has almost fallen over the edge.

THE WRECK OF THE SARGON

In 1947 a British trawler, *Dhoon*, foundered off the Látrabjarg coast in a December storm. Locals scrambled down the frozen cliffs, fired a safety line onto the vessel and winched the seamen to safety. The following year a film crew arrived to make a documentary about the event when another British vessel, *Sargon*, ran aground: the crew were again saved and the whole event was filmed for real.

Hnjótur Museum 9
About 24 km (15 miles) from Látrabjarg, this isolated museum gives an insight into the lives of farmers. Do not miss the video of the *Sargon* shipwreck and the aircraft display.

Breiðavík 10
Breiðavík, 15 km (9 miles) from Látrabjarg, features a long, golden beach **(below)** – a rarity here as the sand is usually volcanic black. On a sunny day you could almost imagine yourself in the Mediterranean.

NEED TO KNOW

MAP A2 ■ Summer-only buses run daily from Ísafjörður. Day returns allow 90 minutes at Látrabjarg. Book in advance: 456 5518; www.wa.is

Visitor Centre: Egils Ólafsson Folk Museum; 456 1511; open Jun–Sep: 10am–6pm daily

Hnjótur Museum: 456 1569; open end-May–mid-Sep: 10am–6pm daily, by appointment at other times; www. westfjords.is

■ The Látrabjarg road is rough gravel, open only in summer. Check your car rental policy. Unless you have experience of similar driving conditions, it is best to take a bus.

■ This area is remote. The hotel at Breiðavík is the nearest place for a meal.

🔟 ⭐ Landmannalaugar Area

Landmannalaugar, meaning "Countryman's Bathing Pool", is a lush hot springs area in southern Iceland, surrounded by a stark wilderness of snow-streaked mountains, ancient lava fields and flat glacial river valleys. Much of the countryside here has been shaped by Hekla, the country's second most active volcano. Excellent camping facilities make it a great spot from which to appreciate the rugged Interior. It is connected by summer-only buses from Reykjavík. You can also hike here along the exceptional Laugavegur trail.

1 Hot Springs
The hot springs emerge into a meadow from underneath a 15th-century lava flow, where they then mingle with a cooler stream. Wade or swim up this stream **(above)** until the water temperature increases, then sit down to enjoy a soak.

2 Mountains
The 945-m- (3,100-ft-) high Bláhnúkur is the main peak overlooking the springs. There is an hour-long trail to its peak. From there you can view the medieval lava field and ever-changing colours of the grey, pink and orange rhyolite hills **(right)**.

3 Ófærufoss
A beautiful, two-stage waterfall **(left)** bridged by lava flowing through what looks like a small volcanic crater. Do not get too close to the rim as the soil is soft.

4 Camp site
The camp site, with grassy spots by the stream and pitches on soft gravel, has showers, toilets and a food preparation area, as well as bins of rocks to weigh down your tent against the infamous gales.

5 Laugavegur
This rewarding, 60-km- (37-mile-) long trail **(below)** from Landmannalaugar to Þórsmörk features volcanic plains, green hills, snowbound plateaus and freezing rivers. You can camp or use bunkhouses for shelter along the way.

6 Flora
Look for tiny, hardy flowers contrasting with the dark lava walls near the springs. Pink thrifts, moss campion, purple self-heals **(left)**, aromatic thyme, white cottongrass and violet butterworts are common.

7 Ljótipollur
Don't let the name, Icelandic for "ugly puddle", put you off visiting this lake, an attractive blue pool inside a bright red scoria depression.

HIKING LAUGAVEGUR

The Laugavegur hike isn't especially difficult but you do need to be self-sufficient and prepared against possible bad conditions. Warm, weatherproof, clothing and hiking boots are necessary, carry maps and a compass, and bring your own food as there are no stores along the way. Bunkhouses must be booked in advance. Campsites are laid out at about 15 km (9 mile) intervals and campers need strong tents in good condition along with cooking gear.

10 Hrafntinnusker
Hrafntinnusker is a huge "reef" made of obsidian (black volcanic glass) located southwest of Landmannalaugar. Look for weathered outcrops around the lava field and on Bláhnúkur, along with smaller pebbles all over.

8 Hekla
The Hekla volcano **(below)**, towering over southwest Iceland, has been erupting at 10-year intervals. The road to Landmannalaugar traverses ash dunes and lava fields from the 1970 eruption *(see p115)*.

9 Frostastaðavatn
Packed with trout, this lake is a favourite fishing spot. The hike around the shore takes 3 hours and it is a fairly easy walk, except for a stretch over a lava field.

NEED TO KNOW

MAP D5 ▪ Mid-Jun–mid-Sep: daily buses from Reykjavík and Skaftafell ▪ www.landmannalaugar.info

Open mid-Jun–late Aug

Book bunkhouses at Landmannalaugar and along Laugavegur hiking trail in advance with the Icelandic Touring Club: www.fi.is

▪ The hot springs can get very busy at weekends and when the Reykjavík bus arrives between 1 and 3pm. Time your soak carefully to avoid the crowds.

▪ In July and early August, you can buy burgers, soft drinks and coffee at the Fjallabúð Café, housed in an old bus at the camp site. There are no other places to eat within 50 km (31 miles).

🔟 ⭐ Jökulsárlón

Jökulsárlón is a broad lagoon on the southeastern coast, where the nose of the Breiðamerkurjökull glacier edges down to the sea. The lagoon formed after the glacier began receding during the 1940s and today presents a striking scene, filled by a mass of icebergs freshly broken off the glacier. With a deep, black-sand beach behind you and the white mass of Europe's largest icecap, Vatnajökull, on the horizon, Jökulsárlón is a great spot to stretch your legs on the long drive from Vík to Höfn.

The Lagoon ①
Around 5 km (3 miles) across and fairly narrow, this is the deepest lagoon in Iceland **(right)**. By contrast, its outflow, the Jökulsá, is the country's shortest river.

② The Beach
Translucent, weirdly shaped boulders of ice **(below)** – the smaller, depleted remains of Jökulsárlón's icebergs – wash downstream to the sea. There they get stranded on the black-sand beach, making for some evocative photographs.

③ Icebergs
The pale blue icebergs create a natural sculpture exhibition, constantly changing shape as they melt, breaking into smaller floes. Eventually they are small enough to float to the sea.

④ Vatnajökull
The lagoon is a good spot to get a feel for Vatnajökull's vast size. Breiðamerkurjökull is 15 km (9 miles) across but even this is only a fraction of the massive white icefield before you (see pp24–5).

⑤ Aquatic Life
Jökulsárlón's cool, deep waters attract herring and trout, which in turn make it a good place to see seals – often spotted snoozing on ice floes **(below)**. Porpoises and other small whales also visit on occasion.

⑥ Breiðárlón
For similar but more remote scenery, head to Breiðárlón, 6 km (4 miles) west along the highway, then 3 km (2 miles) north on a gravel road.

7 In the Movies

Movie buffs may have seen the area even before they visit as it has featured in two Bond films and a Batman film. It is also a popular place to shoot Icelandic TV commercials.

8 Birds

Bird lovers should look out for the ground-nesting Arctic terns **(above)** and the bulkier brown Arctic skuas. Both tend to dive-bomb anything that gets too close to their nests.

BRIDGING THE RIVERS

Bridging the numerous deep, ever-shifting glacial rivers that thread their way seawards all along the south coast was such a massive undertaking that the national highway around the country – the Ringroad – got completed only in 1974. Before this, places like Jökulsárlón were well off the beaten track, as the main road between Skaftafell and Reykjavík was, in reality, just a gravel track.

NEED TO KNOW

MAP G5 ▪ Visitor Centre: 478 2222 ▪ www.vatnajokulsthjodgardur.is ▪ www.jokulsarlon.is

Open Apr–Oct; call ahead to book a boat tour as the timings of the tours can vary

▪ All buses travelling along the south coast of Iceland stop at Jökulsárlón for around 30 minutes, which is long enough to take in the lagoon and walk down to the sea to look at the ice boulders.

▪ The café at the Visitor Centre opens from 9am to 7pm all year round. It serves inexpensive hot food, snacks and coffee. Waffles and seafood soup are specialties.

9 Visitor Centre

Jökulsárlón's small Visitor Centre **(above)** has a café selling fast food and hot drinks, and a few shelves of souvenir postcards and T-shirts. Climb the black hillock out front for great views of the lagoon.

10 Boat Tour

For a chance to enter the maze of icebergs right up against the glacier snout, take a 30-minute amphibious boat tour **(below)** from the Visitor Centre. With a bit of luck, you might also get close to the seals.

The Top 10
of Everything

The northern lights above
the outskirts of Reykjavík

Moments in History

Naddoður discovers Iceland

1 AD 860: Viking Exploration

Around this time a Viking named Naddoður discovered an uninhabited coastline to the northwest of the Faroe Islands. This new land was later visited by the Norseman Flóki Vilgerðarson, who, having spent a harsh winter here, gave it the name "Ísland" (Iceland).

2 AD 870: Reykjavík Settled

Norwegians Ingólfur Arnarson and Hjörleifur Hróðmarsson set sail for Iceland with their families. Hjörleifur was murdered by his slaves after he settled at Hjörleifshöfði. Ingólfur became Iceland's first permanent settler and built his homestead at a place he named Reykjavík ("Smoky Bay").

Statue of Ingólfur Arnarson

3 AD 930: Alþing Established at Þingvellir

All available land in Iceland was settled by AD 930 and regional chieftains found it necessary to form a national government. Rejecting the idea of a king, they opted for a commonwealth. The Parliament (Alþing) was convened annually at Þingvellir, where laws were made and disputes settled.

4 AD 1000: Iceland Becomes Christian

The majority of Iceland's original settlers believed in Norse gods. During the 10th century, however, Norway's king Ólafur Tryggvason threatened Iceland with invasion unless it converted to Christianity. Accordingly, the Alþing of AD 1000 adopted Christianity as Iceland's official religion.

5 1262: The Old Treaty with Norway

During the 13th century, power moved into the hands of wealthy landowners, who plunged the island into civil war. Norway stepped in as peacemaker, and in the year 1262 Iceland accepted Norwegian sovereignty as a semi-independent state under the Old Treaty.

6 1397: Denmark Takes Over

Denmark's ruler, the "Lady King" Margrete, absorbed the Norwegian throne under the Kalmar Union. Later on, Denmark rejected Iceland's claims of autonomy, and in 1661 used military force to impose absolute rule.

7 1550: Iceland Becomes Lutheran

The Danish king appointed Gissur Einarsson as Iceland's first Lutheran bishop in the year 1542. As the nation reluctantly adopted the new faith imposed upon it, Iceland's last Catholic bishop,

Jón Arason, took up arms. He was defeated at Skálholt and executed on 7 November 1550.

8 1783: Lakagígar Eruption

A major volcanic eruption along the Laki craters flooded southeastern Iceland with lava. Poisonous fallout then wiped out agriculture across the land. Famine over the next three years killed one in three Icelanders, and Denmark considered evacuating the entire population to Jutland.

9 1944: Iceland Declares Independence

The mid-19th century saw rising nationalism in Iceland, forcing Denmark to return legislative power to the Alþing in 1874. Nazi Germany's invasion of Denmark during World War II nullified its hold over Iceland, and on 17 June 1944 the country's first president, Sveinn Björnsson, proclaimed Icelandic independence, ending 700 years of foreign rule.

10 2008: Banking Crisis

By the early 2000s, Iceland's agricultural economy had diversified into financial speculation. Icelandic businesses invested in overseas companies, fuelling a credit economy with high interest rates and rapid inflation. When the bubble burst in 2008, the banks collapsed, ruining many and forcing the government to devalue Iceland's currency.

Stained-glass portrait of Jón Arason

TOP 10 FIGURES IN ICELANDIC HISTORY

Plaque honouring Jón Sigurðsson

1 Flóki Vilgerðarson
The Viking who named Iceland and was known as Hrafna-Flóki, or Raven-Flóki, after his pet birds.

2 Ingólfur Arnarson
Iceland's first official settler, who left his native Norway following a feud with the local earl.

3 Leifur Eiríksson
Son of Eirík the Red, Leifur sailed west from Greenland in the year 1000 and discovered America.

4 Guðríður Þorbjarnardóttir
Mother of the first European born in North America, she later made a pilgrimage to Rome.

5 Snorri Sturluson
The 13th-century historian, politician and author of *Egil's Saga*, the *Heimskringla* and the *Prose Edda*.

6 Jón Sigurðsson
Leader of the independence movement, he promoted the move for Iceland's political autonomy from Denmark.

7 Jónas Hallgrímsson
Influential Romantic poet who shaped nationalist pride during the 1800s.

8 Hannes Hafstein
Iceland's first Home Minister in 1904, who oversaw a period of modernization and social change.

9 Vigdís Finnbogadóttir
Iceland's first democratically elected female head of state who served as president from 1980 until 1996.

10 Jóhanna Sigurðardóttir
The world's first openly gay political leader, who served as prime minister of Iceland from 2009 to 2013.

🔟 Churches

1 Dómkirkjan
MAP L2 ■ Austurvöllur Square, Reykjavík ■ 520 9700 ■ Open 10am–4:30pm Mon–Fri

This small, stone and corrugated-iron Lutheran cathedral was built between 1788 and 1796, just as Reykjavík, previously just a collection of farm buildings and warehouses, began to coalesce into Iceland's first town. The unadorned interior shows off the building's simple proportions to beautiful effect.

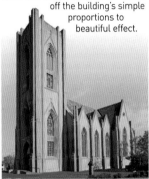

Landakotskirkja cathedral

2 Landakotskirkja
MAP K2 ■ Túngata 15, Reykjavík ■ 552 5388 ■ Open 7:30am–6:30pm daily ■ www. catholica.is

Iceland's Catholic faith was fiercely stomped out in 1550, so it is not surprising that this cathedral dates back to only 1929. Perhaps not to offend Protestant feelings, the building is functional and plain in the extreme and only the entrance and statue of the Virgin Mary give the denomination away.

3 Bænahús at Núpsstaður
MAP E5 ■ Núpsstaður, near Kirkjubæjarklaustur

Wedged below tall cliffs, Núpsstaður is a collection of antique turf farm buildings, including Bænahús church, which was once considered Iceland's remotest holding despite its proximity to the coast. Until the

Bænahús church, Núpsstaður

1850s the nearest harbours were at distant Eyrarbakki and Djúpivogur, and stock had to be transported inland via the highland roads.

4 Grund
MAP E3 ■ Grund, Eyjafjörður

Most unusually for Iceland, this church has an onion-domed cupola topping its wooden tower and Romanesque mini-spires. Though the building is fairly recent – built by trader Magnús Sigurðsson in 1905 – Grund was once a wealthy holding. The treasures of the church include a 15th-century chalice, kept at the National Museum in Reykjavík. The church is privately owned, but visitors are welcome.

Grund church

5 Hallgrímskirkja
Vast in scale as it stands proudly over Reykjavík, Hallgrímskirkja is not a cathedral, although it is Iceland's biggest church. Designed in 1945,

Hallgrímskirkja

8 Þingeyrakirkja

This beautiful stone church in northern Iceland stands close to a Viking assembly site and the presumed location of the country's first monastery. Þingeyrakirkja's medieval alabaster altar was carved in England. The ceiling of the church is painted blue and studded with hundreds of gold stars creating a gorgeous effect *(see p98)*.

construction was undertaken by a family firm of just two people and the building work dragged on, incredibly, until 1986 *(see p76)*.

6 Hóladómkirkja

MAP D2 ▪ Hólar í Hjaltadal ▪ 895 9850 ▪ Open Jun–Sep 10am–6pm daily ▪ Regular buses ▪ www.kirkjan.is/holadomkirkja

Seat of Iceland's second bishopric since the 12th century, this remote cathedral dates to the 1760s, though some sculptures – and the ornate altarpieces – are centuries older. The country's first printing press was founded here in 1530 by Bishop Jón Arason, who is buried in a small adjacent chapel.

7 Skálholtskirkja

MAP C5 ▪ Skálholt, Biskupstungur ▪ 486 8870 ▪ Daily bus from Selfoss, mid-May–Sep; tours from Reykjavík ▪ www.skalholt.is

Iceland's first bishopric, from 1056 until 1801, Skálholt became an important educational centre and at one point was the country's largest settlement. The memorial outside is dedicated to Iceland's last Catholic bishop, Jón Arason, and the 13th-century tomb is that of Bishop Páll Jónsson. Concerts are also sometimes held at the cathedral.

9 Víðimýri

MAP D3 ▪ Víðimýri, Skagafjörður ▪ 453 6173 ▪ Open Jun–Aug 9am–6pm daily ▪ Adm

The 19th-century tiny turf chapel at Víðimýri is one of only six surviving in Iceland, with an attractive timber interior. Check out the walls, weatherproofed by stacking thick slices of earth in a herringbone pattern, and the pretty summertime flowers growing on the grassy roof.

10 Strandakirkja

MAP C5 ▪ Selvogur, near Þorlákshöfn ▪ 483 3771 ▪ Open May–Sep

Standing beyond a small seashore hamlet at the eastern end of the Reykjanes peninsula, Strandakirkja is a picture-perfect 19th-century church, painted pale blue and built on a firm base of square-cut lava blocks. According to local legend, it was funded by grateful sailors who made it ashore at this very spot during a storm.

TOP10 Museums in Reykjavík

1 Listasafn Íslands
National Gallery

A core collection of works by seminal Icelandic artists such as Ásgrímur Jónsson contrasts with avant-garde installations by the likes of Krístján Guðmundsson and Hrafnkell Sigurðsson. The gallery (see p75) showcases regular archaeological and historical exhibitions. It is one of the main venues for the annual Reykjavík Arts Festival in June.

Þjóðminjasafn Íslands

2 Þjóðminjasafn Íslands
National Museum

An exploration of Iceland's history and culture begins with evidence of its earliest visitors (Roman coins found along the south coast), Viking graves, carved doors, medieval church sculptures and 19th-century clothing, and ends with modern pop music and genetic research into the national family tree (see p76).

3 Reykjavík Art Museum

MAP L2 ▪ Hafnarhús, Tryggvagata 17 ▪ 590 1200 ▪ Open 10am–5pm daily, 10am–8pm Thu ▪ Adm (under-18s free); Jun–Aug: free guided tours once a week ▪ www. artmuseum.is

The waterfront branch of the museum's three sites mainly focuses on the Icelandic artist Erró, born in 1932. Of the sculptures, paintings and drawings on display, the most striking are his multicoloured collages of mythical heroes. Another branch focuses on the work of Jóhannes Kjarval (see p76), and the third on Ásmundur Sveinsson (see opposite).

4 Landnámssýningin
Settlement Exhibition

The centrepiece to this excellent subterranean museum is the oval foundation wall of a Viking long-house, with a distinctive underlying layer of volcanic ash, dated AD 871. Holographic dioramas and artifacts, including wooden farm implements and corroded axes, bring it all to life. Look for sacrificial cow bones among the foundations (see p75).

5 The Einar Jónsson Sculpture Museum

Einar Jónsson's pieces owe a good deal to the early 20th-century national-ist movements across Europe, with heroic figures in dramatic, iconic arrangements. One of the favourites is St George resting on his sword, holding his shield aloft, with the dragon coiling behind (see p78).

Sculpture by Einar Jónsson

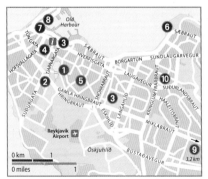

6 Sigurjón Ólafsson Sculpture Museum

Located along the foreshore, this gallery was founded by the artist's widow. It displays Sigurjón's modernist, abstract works in timber, stone and metal, ranging from smoothly contoured sculptures to giant installations looking like totem poles made out of scrap iron and driftwood *(see p78)*.

A stone sculpture by Sigurjón Ólafsson

7 The Saga Museum

MAP Q5 ■ Grandagardi 2 ■ 511 1517 ■ Open 10am–6pm daily ■ Adm ■ www.sagamuseum.is

This hugely enjoyable museum features characters from the Icelandic sagas, including larger-than-life Vikings such as the violent but gifted Egil Skallagrímsson, Leif Eiríksson, discoverer of America, and the ill-fated poet, politician and saga author Snorri Sturluson. There is realistic detail in the clothing and period buildings, as well as the vivid Viking-age noises and smells.

8 Reykjavík Maritime Museum

MAP K1 ■ Grandagarður 8, 101 Reykjavík ■ 411 6340 ■ Open 10am–5pm daily ■ Adm ■ www.maritimemuseum.is

This museum at Reykjavík's old harbour tries to convey a flavour of life on the ocean. Pick of the exhibits is the magnificent *Óðinn*, a coastguard vessel docked at the museum's pier.

Óðinn, Reykjavík Maritime Museum

9 Árbæjarsafn

MAP P6 ■ Kistuhyl 4, Árbær ■ 411 6300 ■ Bus 12, 19 or 24 from Hlemmur & Lækjartorg ■ Open Jun–Aug: 10am–5pm daily; Sep–May: guided tours only 1pm or by appointment ■ Adm ■ www.minjasafnreykjavikur.is

A former farm has been converted into an open-air museum of old buildings, farm machinery and period artifacts. The best permanent exhibit is the turf-roofed timber house from the late 19th century. Regular events, when the machinery is fired up and domestic animals wander around, bring the place to life.

Árbæjarsafn shows a bygone lifestyle

10 Ásmundur Sveinsson Sculpture Museum

Part of the Reykjavík Art Museum, this building is an attraction in itself, but the real pleasure is walking around the sculpture garden outside, full of Ásmundur's powerful depiction of themes from history and folklore, influenced by Cubism and African tribal art. Inside are smaller pieces in a variety of media *(see p78)*.

🔟 Museums Around Iceland

1 Borgarnes Settlement Center

The museum is in two halves and its entry price includes audio guides (in 14 languages). Upstairs, Iceland's settlement is covered in detail, from a pneumatic longship prow to impressions of how the islands looked with more trees and no sheep. Downstairs, *Egil's Saga* is brought to life with carvings of key scenes from this violent tale *(see p83)*.

Carving of Egil's Saga

2 Icelandic Emigration Centre

MAP D2 ■ Hofsós ■ 453 7935 ■ Buses in summer ■ Open Jun–Aug: 11am–6pm daily ■ Adm ■ www.hofsos.is

The lonely setting of this museum on the north coast gives some idea of the feelings endured by the thousands of 19th-century Icelanders who left for Canada following a catastrophic series of harsh winters and volcanic eruptions.

3 Skógar Museum

MAP D6 ■ Skógar ■ 487 8845 ■ Buses from Reykjavík and Höfn ■ Open May & Sep: 10am–5pm daily; Jun–Aug: 9am–6pm daily; Oct–Apr: 11am–4pm daily ■ Adm ■ www.skogasafn.is

The museum's collection documents over 1,000 years of history. There is a brass ring off a Viking treasure chest, traditional turf buildings, a

Skógar Museum

Bible from 1584 (Iceland's first printed book), an eight-oared fishing boat and traditional clothing.

Herring Era Museum

4 Herring Era Museum

MAP D2 ■ Snorragata 15, Siglufjörður ■ 467 1604 ■ Buses in summer ■ Open Jun–Aug: 10am–6pm daily; Sep–May: 1–5pm daily ■ Adm ■ www.sild.is

Increasingly popular with tourists today, Siglufjörður was once – until fish stocks fell in the 1960s – Iceland's busiest herring port, its harbour crammed with boats. The award-winning museum documents those hectic times in photos, models and dioramas, including photos of the "herring girls" who cleaned and salted the catches. On Saturdays there is a live outdoor salting show.

5 Orkusýn Geothermal Energy Exhibition

MAP C5 ■ Hellisheiði Power Plant, 20 mins drive from Reykjavík towards Hveragerði on Route 1 ■ Open 9am–5pm daily ■ Adm ■ www.orkusyn.is

The state-of-the-art exhibition shows how geothermal energy is used in Iceland and its potential as a nonpolluting energy source. The guided tour is excellent and the interactive multimedia exhibits are fascinating as well, especially the earthquake simulator – although it is definitely not for the faint-hearted.

6 Húsavík Whale Museum

MAP E2 ▪ Hafnarstétt 1, Húsavík ▪ 414 2800 ▪ Open Apr, May & Sep: 9am–4pm daily; Jun–Aug: 8:30am–6:30pm daily; Oct–Mar: 10am–3:30pm Mon–Fri ▪ Adm ▪ www.whalemuseum.is

Overlooking Húsavík harbour, where whaling boats are now used for whale-watching tours, this museum uses videos, relics and whole minke and humpback skeletons to provide information on whales. It is essential viewing before heading seawards to see the whales in the flesh.

7 Icelandic Museum of Rock & Roll

MAP B5 ▪ Hjallavegur 2, 260 Reykjanesbær ▪ 420 1030 ▪ Open 11am–6pm daily ▪ Adm (under-16s free) ▪ www.rokksafn.is

The museum documents the story of Icelandic rock and pop music, covering the likes of Sigur Rós and Björk. Visitors can borrow iPads so they can listen to featured artists' music, check out the Icelandic Music Hall of Fame and try out instruments in the Sound Lab.

8 Langabúð

MAP G4 ▪ Djúpivogur ▪ 478 8220 ▪ Buses run between Höfn and Egilsstaðir in summer ▪ Open Jun–Sep: 10am–6pm daily ▪ Adm

The oldest wooden building on Djúpivogur harbour, Langabúð was built as a warehouse in 1790 and is now a cultural centre, folk museum and memorial to local artist Ríkarður Jónsson (1888–1977) who taught drawing and sculpture. His works are on display here. It also has a coffee shop.

Húsavík Whale Museum

9 Westfjords Maritime Museum

MAP B2 ▪ Turnhús, Suðurgata, Ísafjörður ▪ 896 3291 ▪ Open mid-May–mid-Sep: 9am–5pm daily ▪ Adm ▪ www.nedsti.is

Ísafjörður was settled in the 1580s and later became a busy port for saltfish. This museum, located in the town's 18th-century Turnhús (the towerhouse was a lookout post), documents those times. Photos show the town centre has changed little since the early 20th century.

10 Viking World

MAP B5 ▪ Víkingabraut 1, 260 Reykjanesbær ▪ 422 2000 ▪ Open summer: 11am–6pm daily; winter: noon–5pm daily ▪ Adm ▪ www.vikingaheimar.is

The modern, glass-sided museum just outside Keflavík houses the Íslendingur, a full-scale reproduction of a wooden Viking longship unearthed in Norway in the 1880s. Íslendingur was built by Captain Gunnar Marel Eggertsson, who sailed in it to New York in 2000 to celebrate the millennium of the Viking discovery of North America.

Waterfalls

Water splashing from under the moss-covered lava bank, Hraunfossar

1 Dettifoss
MAP F2

Europe's biggest waterfall in terms of volume, this monster at Jökulsárgljúfur National Park in northeastern Iceland can be heard miles away. The stark setting, where the river drops 45 m (148 ft) between the shattered cliffs of the Jökulsá canyon, adds to the spectacle. Upstream is another waterfall, Selfoss, only 10 m (33 ft) high but 70 m (230 ft) across.

2 Glymur
MAP C4

Iceland's tallest waterfall, Glymur drops nearly 200 m (658 ft) off the top of a plateau inland from Hvalfjörður, along the west coast. Legend has it that a mythical beast, half-man and half-whale, swam up the waterfall and into Hvalvatn, the lake at the top – where whale bones have indeed been found.

3 Gullfoss

This large, beautiful and always impressive two-tier fall sits on the Hvítá river around 75 km (47 miles) northeast of Reykjavík. It is one of Iceland's most visited sights, along with nearby Geysir and Þingvellir. In the early 20th century it was at the heart of the country's first environmental dispute (see pp18–19).

4 Seljalandsfoss
MAP D6

Fed by the melting water from Eyjafjallajökull icecap, Seljalandsfoss is narrow and not especially tall, but it drops into a meadow along the south coast with surprising force. Adventurous visitors can take a walk along the path behind the water curtain, for a good soak. Look out for several smaller falls nearby.

5 Hraunfossar and Barnafoss
MAP C4

Two adjacent falls within easy reach of Borgarnes on the west coast, with very different characters. At Hraunfossar, blue water splashes out from under a moss-covered lava bank and gurgles down into the river, while Barnafoss forms a short, savage set of rapids as it cuts through a narrow canyon just upstream.

6 Skógafoss
MAP D6

Just walking up along the river to this mighty waterfall is an incredible experience: as you approach, the flat gravel plain vanishes inside soaking clouds of spray and an extraordinary level of noise. Climb a staircase up to the top for more cascades and views out over southern Iceland's coastline.

The cascades of Skógafoss

7 Dynjandi
MAP B2

This waterfall in the Westfjords near Hrafnseyri cascades over several tiers of basalt boulders in a 60-m- (198-ft-) wide, 100-m (329-ft) drop. Crashing over all those boulders gives Dynjandi ("the Thunderer") its name, but views seawards over grassy dales make it a beautiful place to camp out.

8 Goðafoss
MAP E2

Located between Akureyri and Mývatn, this "Waterfall of the Gods" is where the 10th-century Law-speaker Þorgeir Ljósvetningagoði, who championed the introduction of Christianity to Iceland, disposed of the statues of pagan Norse gods in the year 1000. The ice-blue water channels over several falls, with easy walking tracks between them.

9 Aldeyjarfoss
MAP E3

Off the northern end of the rugged Sprengisandur Route across Iceland's Interior, Aldeyjarfoss cuts a rough scar across the huge Suðurárhraun lava field, exposing layers of ash and rock that have settled over successive eruptions. Although only 20 m (66 ft) high, the falls are very forceful and perk up an otherwise lifeless terrain.

10 Ófærufoss
MAP E5

This waterfall is associated with the Eldgjá canyon on the Fjallabak Route between Landmannalaugar and Skaftafell. The river flows along the top and drops into the canyon, gouging out a broad, scree-ridden pool before falling again as a smaller curtain onto the plain.

Aldeyjarfoss, at the north end of the Sprengisandur Route

Volcanoes

Ash cloud rising from Eyjafjallajökull

1 Hekla

This large, lively mountain has erupted over a dozen times since Iceland was settled, most famously burying a host of nearby Viking farms under ash in 1104. The last major stirrings were in the 1940s, but there have been many smaller incidents since then. In between eruptions, experienced hikers can walk to the top (see p115).

2 Eyjafjallajökull
MAP D6

In March 2010, an eruption of the Eyjafjallajökull volcano began at the Fimmvörðuháls hiking trail (see p60). A month later, as it petered out, a much bigger eruption started in the main crater of the volcano. From the 4th until the 20th of April, a vast cloud of volcanic ash spread across large areas of Europe. Many countries closed their airspace, affecting hundreds of thousands of passengers. A visitor centre at the base of the volcano, at Þorvaldseyri, shows films of the eruption.

3 Snæfell
MAP A4

This stratovolcano – one whose cone has built up gradually over successive eruptions – is believed to have last erupted around AD 250 and today is covered by the Snæfellsjökull icecap (see pp26–7). Unlike Hekla, whose top is usually shrouded by cloud, Snæfell's bright white peak stands like a beacon over the west coast of the country.

4 Öræfajökull
MAP F5

Iceland's tallest volcano is located near Ingólfshöfði. Its terrible explosion in 1362 buried almost a third of the country under gravel and forced the abandonment of farms all along the south coast. Another eruption in 1727 caused less damage, mainly because only a few people had returned to live here.

Lakagígar, southern Iceland

5 Lakagígar

In 1783, the countryside inland from Kirkjubæjarklaustur split open a huge rent, which belched fire and poisonous fumes for seven months. It is said that Kirkjubæjarklaustur itself was saved by the actions of pastor Jón Steingrímsson, who bundled the town's population into the church and prayed that they be spared – the lava halted right at the church boundary (see p116).

6 Eldfell
MAP C6

The 1973 eruption of Eldfell on Heimaey, in the Westman Islands, buried a third of the town under lava and the rest under ash. But the harbour was saved – and even improved – by the spraying of seawater onto the lava front as it edged down from the volcano.

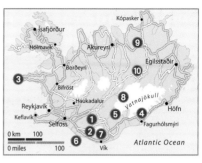

7 Katla
MAP D6

This dangerous volcano lies buried beneath the Mýrdalsjökull icecap near Skógar on the south coast. It erupts on average at a 70-year interval, and the last one, in 1918, sent a titanic flood of meltwater and gravel down nearby valleys. Recent activity in the area, including earthquakes in the caldera, might be signalling an awakening.

8 Grímsvötn
MAP E4

Currently Iceland's most active volcano, Grímsvötn smoulders away 400 m (1,315 ft) below the massive Vatnajökull icecap. A massive *jökulhlaup* – a volcanically induced flash flood – tore out from under the Skeiðarárjökull glacier in 1995, destroying several bridges. There was another eruption in May 2011.

9 Krafla

The Krafla Fires of 1975–84, northeast of Mývatn, happened at a bad time: they delayed the completion of the Leirbotn Geothermal Power Station, under construction at the time, for over a decade. However, the new source of natural heat might make it possible to increase the station's projected 60 MW output (see p21).

10 Askja
MAP F3

In 1875, a small vent in the Askja caldera exploded with such force that it vaporized 2 cubic km (1 cubic mile) of rock, burying farms across northeastern Iceland in a thick layer of pumice and sparking mass emigration to Canada. Askja last erupted in 1961, but the current eruption of Bárðabunga at Holuhraun is connected to the system.

Askja, northeastern Iceland

TOP 10 Hot Springs and Geysers

Geothermal spa water at the Blue Lagoon

1 Geysir

Now just a flooded crater at the top of a mound, Geysir once set the benchmark for erupting hot spouts worldwide (giving them their name) until its subterranean vents became clogged with debris. A big earthquake in 2008 might have cleared some of them: new bubbling and hissing are the first signs of action for decades (see pp16–17).

2 Jarðböðin Nature Baths

This mineral-rich natural spa uses its dramatic location on a steaming volcanic ridge overlooking Lake Mývatn to good effect. Take a look across the road too, where people have dug pits in the hot soil, covered them with metal lids, and use them as ovens for baking bread – and cooking sheep heads (see p21).

Jarðböðin Nature Baths

3 The Blue Lagoon

Only Icelanders could turn the outflow from a geothermal power station into the country's premier tourist attraction. At the Blue Lagoon they have done a superb job, even if the first thing you see when you arrive is people emerging from the milky-blue water with their faces covered in the fine white silt that is also sold here as a beauty product (see pp14–15).

4 Deildartunguhver
MAP C4

Water emerging at 97°C (207°F) at Deildartunguhver, Europe's largest hot spring, fills the skies with steam near the historic hamlet of Reykholt in the west of Iceland. There is no bathing pool here – the water is pumped straight to the coastal towns of Borgarnes and Akranes – but the violently spluttering vent is an impressive sight in itself.

5 Landmannalaugar

Popular with Icelanders and tourists alike, Landmannalaugar is the country's finest natural bathing pool – you just can't beat the feeling of soaking away in the hot stream here as a wall of lava towers overhead and fractured orange mountains frame the distance. No other part of the Interior is so wild, yet so accessible (see pp30–31).

Strokkur erupts

sulphur-rich orange plain stretching away to the south of the hillside, only adds to the impression.

9 Hveravellir
MAP D4 ■ Summer buses from Reykjavík and Akureyri ■ Bus schedules: www.bsi.is

A famous hot spring on the Kjölur route across the Interior, this was once used by the 17th-century outlaw Eyvindur for warmth and to cook stolen sheep. A great spot to pause during the rough, 5-hour ride from Gullfoss to Akureyri and enjoy a soak in the cooler spa pool alongside the hot spring.

10 Hengill
MAP R6

This is a popular hiking area west of Hveragerði, with hot springs and steam vents. Many of these springs and vents are being diverted for geothermal energy projects – power plants and miles of silver-coloured pipes for Reykjavík's water and electricity supplies are visible nearby.

Seltún, on the Reykjanes peninsula

6 Strokkur
Geysir's stand-in, Strokkur *(see pp16–17),* is far more reliable too, erupting 10 times in an hour – even at its peak, Geysir often lay quiet for days at a time. Strokkur is the largest continually active geyser in Iceland (and the one featured in most photographs), reaching impressive heights on a good day.

7 Seltún
MAP B5

Down on the Reykjanes peninsula near Reykjavík, there was a decent geyser at Seltún in Krýsuvík, until the entire spring exploded in 1999, leaving behind a grey, bubbling pool. But smaller hot springs still seep out of the hills above, making for an interesting half-hour walk – do not leave the marked paths.

8 Námaskarð
This hillside to the east of Lake Mývatn, dotted with roaring steam vents and coloured mud pools, does a fantastic job of demonstrating what a raw and powerful force nature can be *(see p21).* The setting, with a lonely,

🔟 Offshore Islands

Imagine Peace Tower, Viðey

1 Viðey
MAP P5 ■ Daily ferries from Reykjavík ■ www.videy.com

Key historical figures have settled on this flat speck of land just off Reykjavík, among them the country's last Catholic bishop, Jón Arason, and sheriff Skúli Magnússon, who built Iceland's first stone house here in 1755. Today it is a stage for the circular Imagine Peace Tower in memory of John Lennon.

2 Lundey
MAP P5 ■ Cruises from Reykjavík ■ www.elding.is

There are plenty of places called Lundey around Iceland – the name means "Puffin Island" – but this is the closest spot to Reykjavík where you can actually see the birds in question, at least while they are nesting between April and August. You cannot land here, but cruises circle Lundey daily in summer.

3 Vigur
MAP B2 ■ Daily ferry from Ísafjörður mid-Jun–late Aug ■ www.vesturferdir.is

Out in the Westfjords, this remote elongated islet makes a great half-day trip from Ísafjörður to see Arctic terns, puffins and especially eider ducks, whose warm, insulating down is commercially gathered for stuffing duvets and jackets. Only discarded chest feathers are collected and the birds are not harmed.

One of Vigur's eider ducks

4 Hrísey
MAP E2 ■ Daily ferry from Árskógssandur ■ www.visitakureyri.is

Up on the north coast near Akureyri, this island is famous for the colossal number of wild, but completely tame, ptarmigans that live here. Though common all over Iceland, these birds can be rare in some years, so this is where to come if you have been unable to see them elsewhere.

A puffin on Grímsey

5 Grímsey

MAP E1 ■ Ferry safari from Dalvík Mon–Wed, Fri at 9am; many flights a week from Akureyri ■ www.akureyri.is/grimsey-en/grimsey-island

Iceland's northernmost point and the only part actually crossed by the Arctic Circle – meaning the sun really does not set here for a few days either side of 21 June and does not rise at all in late December. The island's cliffs are full of seabirds. A great day-trip destination.

6 Papey

MAP H4 ■ Daily ferry from Djúpivogur Jun–Aug

Papey ("Monks' Island") is named after the Christian hermits who are believed to have been living here when the Vikings arrived in Iceland. Today the 2 sq km (1 sq mile) island, rising just 60 m (197 ft) out of the sea, is home to thousands of puffins, a few sheep and the smallest church in the country.

7 Flatey

MAP E2 ■ Daily ferry from Stykkishólmur–Brjánslækur ■ www.seatours.is

Although hard to believe, this sleepy island, halfway across Breiðafjörður between Snæfellsnes and the Westfjords, housed an important 12th-century monastery. Later it became famous for the *Flateyjarbók*, an illuminated medieval manuscript featuring the *Greenland Saga*, now kept in Reykjavík's Culture House. The east of the island is a reserve for nesting seabirds.

8 Heimaey

MAP C6 ■ Daily ferry to Herjólfur from Þorlákshöfn or Landeyjahöfn mid-May–mid-Sep; flights from Reykjavík and Bakki ■ www.eimskip.is

This 3-km- (2-mile-) long island off the south coast has enough birds, volcanoes, Viking history and walks to occupy you for a couple of sunny days. The town of the same name occupies the north end of the island and is famous for being nearly annihilated during a volcanic eruption in 1973.

9 Eldey

MAP B5

About 15 km (9 miles) off Iceland's southwesternmost tip, Eldey's distinctive, rocky, sheer-sided cliffs rise 77 m (250 ft) straight out of the Atlantic. The top forms a level platform, home to Europe's largest gannet colony. Sadly, this is also where the last known pair of great auks were killed in 1844.

10 Surtsey

MAP C6

Surtsey dramatically popped out of the waves during an underwater volcanic eruption to the southwest of Heimaey in 1963. Following erosion over the years, the island is now around 1.5 km (1 mile) across. Scientists are studying Surtsey to see how plants and animals colonize new lands. It is a special UNESCO reserve and strictly off-limits.

Heimaey, picturesque island town

🔟 Places to See Birds and Wildlife

1 Lake Mývatn

The country's top venue for viewing wildlife, Lake Mývatn slots easily into a trip to see Iceland's laid-back northern capital, Akureyri, and a whale-watching expedition from Húsavík. Ducks and other wildfowl are the main draws, but the elusive Arctic fox and gyrfalcon are also regularly encountered *(see pp20–21)*.

2 Látrabjarg

Way out in the Westfjords, a trip to Látrabjarg takes a little bit of planning but you will not forget your first sight of these cliffs, covered by enormous, noisy colonies of nesting seabirds. Stop along the way for a walk or sunbathe on Breiðavík beach *(see pp28–9)*.

Hornbjarg, on isolated Hornstrandir

3 Hornbjarg
MAP B1

At 533 m (1,749 ft), Hornbjarg is the highest clifftop on the isolated, completely uninhabited Hornstrandir peninsula, on the Westfjords' extreme northwest. Like Látrabjarg, it is teeming with fulmars, kitti-wakes, razorbills and guillemots. There are regular guided day tours, as well as other scheduled boat trips, from Ísafjörður.

4 Dyrhólaey
MAP D6 ■ Closed 7pm–9am

The headland of Dyrhólaey is an easy detour off the highway between Skógar and Vík (there are restrictions on cars but it is open for hiking). Apart from puffins and other seabirds, come here to view the black, volcanic-sand beaches and the huge sea arch, large enough for a ship to sail through.

Skua, Dyrhólaey

5 Jökulsárlón

One of the most spellbinding sights of southeastern Iceland, this deep, iceberg-filled lagoon between the sea and Breiðamerkurjökull glacier is a great place to spot seals and orca, if you are lucky. The sandy plains on either side are full of nesting terns and skuas – and arctic foxes looking for a meal *(see pp32–3)*.

6 Skjálfandi
MAP E2

A summer sailing trip out from Húsavík to Skjálfandi, the broad bay offshore, is certain to put you within viewing range of marine mammals. You are most likely to see seals and dolphins but with luck you will encounter the spectacular hump-back whales leaping out of the water.

Humpback whale at Skjálfandi

7 Breiðafjörður
MAP B3

The waters off the west coast are dotted with hundreds of islets and skerries inhabited by thousands of puffins, shags, cormorants and other seabirds. White-tailed sea eagles, one of Iceland's rarest, most majestic species, are also seen here.

8 Garðskagi
MAP B5

Close to Keflavík International Airport, this little tongue of land overlooks a gravelly beach where you can easily spot redshanks, sanderlings, turnstones, eider duck and other shorebirds – look out to sea for gannets. The striped red lighthouse was once used to monitor bird migration.

Garðskagi lighthouse

9 Ingólfshöfði
MAP F5 ■ Hofsnes Farm ■ 894 0894 ■ Tractor tours: Apr–Oct daily at 9am, noon & 3pm; book online at www.localguide.is ■ Adm

This spit of land between Vík and Höfn is said to be where Iceland's first settler, Ingólfur Arnarson, landed. Puffins and great skua nest here in the summer, when tractor tours trundle out from the highway.

10 Jökulsá á Dal
MAP G3 ■

With river systems and integrated wetlands merging from the highland moors around Snæfell down to the East Fjords coast, this is a summer breeding ground for geese, swans and all manner of wildfowl. Keep an eye open for reindeer herds too.

TOP 10 ICELANDIC BIRDS

Ptarmigan

1 Puffin
This charismatic bird nests in burrows on grassy sea cliffs around Iceland between May and September.

2 Arctic Tern
A small, graceful seabird that fearlessly dive-bombs anything that gets too close to its nest.

3 Gyrfalcon
A rare, grey-white falcon that once featured on Iceland's coat of arms. Seek it out around Mývatn Lake.

4 Golden Plover
Common grassland bird whose piping call is eagerly awaited by Icelanders as heralding the spring.

5 Raven
Huge black crow with a harsh call and acrobatic flight, considered highly intelligent by many Icelanders.

6 Meadow Pipit
The island's most abundant bird is a sweet songster, though it can be surprisingly hard to see.

7 White-tailed Sea Eagle
Once persecuted by farmers as a pest, around 80 white-tailed sea eagles now breed in the northwest.

8 Eider Duck
Pied sea duck known for its soft, warm down. It is common around the coast and on lakes inland.

9 Ptarmigan
Grouse renowned for its unique, snow-white winter plumage. A popular Christmas dish in Iceland.

10 Harlequin Duck
This sea duck has an unmistakable blue and red plumage. It breeds inland from May until July around fast-flowing streams.

Things to Do With Kids

One of many heated outdoor pools

1 Go Swimming
Swimming pools are great places for children to burn off any excess energy, especially after a long car journey. Just about every town in Iceland has a heated pool, which makes it an easy option. Though most of the pools are outdoors, they are especially fun in winter, when snow is falling.

2 Feed the Birds at Tjörnin
In Reykjavík, pick up a loaf of bread from the nearest bakery and head to Tjörnin lake in the centre of the city (see p78) to feed whooper swans, greylag geese, mallards and eider ducks – in June and July there are a lot of cute ducklings around too. Just watch out for pushy seagulls trying to muscle in.

A child feeds the birds at Tjörnin, in central Reykjavík

3 Visit the Museums
Iceland's most engaging museums for children are the open-air Árbæjarsafn museum of traditional farm life (see p41); the Saga Centre at Hvolsvöllur, full of swords and dioramas (see p112); Borgarnes Settlement Center, showcasing spooky recreations of Egil's Saga (see p42); and Húsavík Whale Museum (see p43), with its fascinating skeletons and marine mammal displays.

4 Eat a Hot Dog
MAP L2 ■ Tryggvagata, 101 Reykjavík

Eating a pylsur (hot dog) from the flagship Bæjarins Beztu wagon in central Reykjavík (there are three further stands around the city) is a rite of passage for young Icelanders, who form long queues outside this unpretentious mobile stand. Why? The hot dogs taste great – though you might want to hold the onions.

5 Visit Reykjavík Harbour
MAP K1

Reykjavík has a busy harbour, with all types of colourful fishing boats and trawlers sailing in and out on a daily basis or hauled up on slipways for repairs. Look in the waters and you might also see jellyfish. Snack along nearby Geirsgata at either Búllan (see p64) for burgers, or at Icelandic Fish & Chips (see p65) on Tryggvagata.

6 Go Horse Riding
Short and stocky Icelandic horses are even-tempered, making them child-friendly and a good choice for first-timers. Most of the riding schools cater to children with their flexible schedules and duration of rides (see p50).

7 Picnic at Reykjavík Botanic Gardens
The botanical gardens make for a pleasant place for a family outing

and picnic, just a short way from downtown Reykjavík *(see p77)*. There is plenty of soft grass, ducks and geese wandering about, and – in the summertime at least – beds of colourful endemic flowers. Don't miss the small zoo, which is full of native mammals and birds.

8 Enjoy Whale-Watching
In Iceland there is quite a good chance of seeing minke and humpback whales, orca, sperm whales and even exciting rarities like blue whales. Húsavík *(see p96)* is the best place to go whale-watching.

9 Hunt for Trolls
Trolls, the frightening, mischief-making giants, are said in local folklore to inhabit several places in Iceland. They turn to stone if they are caught in the sunlight but their oddly shaped, petrified forms can be seen (if you look hard enough) in many lava fields, mountain outcrops and sea stacks.

A rusted shipwreck in Reykjanes

10 Go Beachcombing
Icelandic beaches are full of interesting flotsam and jetsam, from bird feathers and oddly shaped pebbles to rusted relics from shipwrecks, tree trunks (which have floated here from Siberia) and even – if you are really lucky – whale bones.

TOP 10 ICELANDIC FOLKTALES

Statue of Smundur the Wise

1 Eyvindur and Halla
Iceland's most famous medieval outlaw, along with his wife, Halla, survived 20 years on the run.

2 Viking Treasure at Skógafoss
Legend has it that a Viking named Þrasi Þórólfsson hid his hoarded gold in a cave behind the Skógafoss waterfall.

3 The Beast of Hvalfjörður
This evil, red-headed whale terrorized Iceland's west coast until it was lured into a trap.

4 Ormurinn, the Lagarfljót Serpent
Iceland's elusive version of the Loch Ness Monster is said to inhabit Lögurinn Lake near Egilsstaðir in the east of the country.

5 Bergþór
A friendly giant who lived at Bláfell, near Geysir, and died around 1000.

6 The Lovestruck Shepherd
A favourite tale about a young man who waded across the Hvítá river to propose to a shepherdess.

7 Sæmundur the Wise
Founder of an 11th-century ecclesiastical school, who frequently took on and always defeated the Devil.

8 The Origin of Öxará Falls
Said to have been created around AD 930 when the Öxará river at Þingvellir was diverted.

9 Were-Seals
Seals are thought to sometimes adopt human form, especially those that swim close to shore.

10 Snorri
The wily thief Snorri escaped pursuit inside a small cave at Þórsmörk – it is near the bus stop.

Following pages Interior of Harpa, Reykjavík Concert Hall and Conference Centre

🔟 Outdoor Activities

Hikers on the Laugavegur trail

① Hiking
Hiking organizations: www.fi.is; www.utivist.is; www. mountainguides.is

Nothing gets you closer to Iceland's raw, natural landscape than hiking across it, following established trails ranging in length from an hour to a week. The pick of these are at Landmannalaugar, Jökulsárgljúfur, Skaftafell and Þórsmörk, where you can navigate grassy meadows with wildflowers, lava fields, black-sand deserts and icefields.

② Swimming
Just about every Icelandic town has an outdoor geothermal swimming pool heated to 28°C (82°F), always with accompanying "hot pot" tubs at 34–38°C (93–100°F), and sometimes with saunas and water slides.

③ Horse Riding
Riding centres: www.eldhestar. is; www.ishestar.is

Iceland's specific breed of horses arrived with the Vikings. Though lacking the size and speed of Arab horses, they have a unique gliding gait, called the *tölt*, which is used for moving softly over the rough Icelandic terrain. Many riding schools and farms offer excursions.

④ Fishing
www.icelandangling.com

Recreational deep-sea angling is in its infancy here and most people fly-fish for trout, salmon or char. A permit is essential: those for trout and char are easy to pick up on the spot, but for salmon you need to apply in advance.

⑤ River Rafting
www.arcticrafting.is

What Iceland's rivers may lack in size they more than make up for in drama. They tear through narrow volcanic gorges, forming lively rapids. Two of the longest rivers in the country – the Þjórsá and the Hvítá – are accessible for white-water rafting, with trips available during the summer.

⑥ Snowmobiling
www.glacierjeeps.is

Snowmobiling or Skidooing is an expensive but exhilarating way to tear across snowfields and glaciers at 40 kmph (25 mph). The best place to try it is at Skálafellsjökull, an outrunner of Vatnajökull.

⑦ Jeep Touring
www.glacierjeeps.is

The harsh Interior – a spread of rough lava fields, gigantic icecaps and gravel plains braided by glacial rivers – is navigable only by high-clearance 4WDs. Public buses fit the bill and many private operators offer tours in off-road Jeeps.

Horse riding on Snæfellsnes peninsula

8 Skiing and Snowboarding

www.skidasvaedi.is

There are established winter skiing and snowboarding venues around Reykjavík, Akureyri, Hlíðarfjall and in the Westfjords, complete with bunkhouses, ski lifts and graded runs. The most accessible are Bláfjöll, outside Reykjavík, and the popular summer slopes at west Snæfellsjökull, with winter cross-country opportunities around Mývatn.

Iceland offers many skiing venues

9 Scuba Diving

MAP C5 ■ www.dive.is; www.diveiceland.com

There are several areas to scuba dive in Iceland – the most popular are Silfra and other spots around Þingvallavatn. With crystal-clear, pale blue water and submerged lava formations, Silfra is rated as one of the best freshwater sites in the world.

10 Aurora Borealis Watching

The northern lights, or aurora borealis, are solar particles fluorescing as they stream across the upper atmosphere, appearing as luminous curtains of colour. They are best viewed on cold nights in years of heavy solar activity, away from sources of light pollution. Ideal conditions occur between November and February.

TOP 10 PLACES TO BATHE AND SWIM

Bathing in the Blue Lagoon

1 The Blue Lagoon
Surreal blue water, steam and black lava boulders feature at this ultimate bathing hotspot (see pp14–15).

2 Laugardalur
Reykjavík's best public pool, complete with separate children's play pool and a steam room (see p77).

3 Borgarnes
MAP B4 ■ Open 7am–9pm Mon–Fri, 9am–6pm Sat & Sun ■ Adm
The town's swimming pool has exceptional views from the water.

4 Landmannalaugar
Natural hot springs surrounded by lava walls and orange and grey rhyolite mountains (see pp30–31).

5 Jarðböðin
Mývatn's answer to the Blue Lagoon, set up on a hillside among live volcanic scenery (see p21).

6 Selárdalslaug
MAP G2 ■ Open 10am–10pm daily
Tiny public pool near Vopnafjörður, beside the fast-flowing green waters of the Selá river.

7 Krossneslaug
Unforgettable hot springs and a bathing pool in the north, near Norðurfjörður (see p91).

8 Hofsós
MAP D2
The waterline of this seaside pool appears to merge with the ocean.

9 Grettislaug
Remote natural hot tub in the northwest, bathing place of Viking outlaw Grettir (see p95).

10 Laugarvatn
MAP C5 ■ Open 10am–9pm Mon–Fri, 10am–6pm Sat & Sun ■ Adm
Huge outdoor pool at the National School for Sports near Geysir.

Hiking Trails

View along the coastal trail from Arnarstapi to Hellnar

1 Arnarstapi to Hellnar
MAP A4

This short coastal walk between the two small villages offers great seascapes and views of Snæfellsjökull's white cone. Along the way look out for the statue of Bárður Snæfellsás and nesting Arctic terns.

2 Esja
MAP Q5

Esja's 914-m- (2,999-ft-) high plateau rises unmistakably above the bay north of Reykjavík. Its snow-streaked slopes appear to mutate with the changing light – the colours shift from deep brown to pale blue. A return hike from the Mógilsá forestry station takes about 4 hours.

3 Fimmvörðuháls
MAP D6 ■ Summer buses to Skógar and Þórsmörk ■ Trail open mid-Jun–Sep ■ www.fi.is

An overnight trek from Skógar to Þórsmörk can be done separately or as an extension to the Laugavegur

Start of Fimmvörðuháls trail, Skógar

trail. From Skógar, climb the steps to the top of the waterfall and follow the river upstream to cross the pass between Eyjafjallajökull (see p46) and Mýrdalsjökull icecaps, before descending to Þórsmörk.

4 Þingvellir
MAP C5 ■ Daily buses from Reykjavík

The mossy valley floor of Þingvellir is crisscrossed by easy hiking trails of 1 to 3 hours in duration. Stick to the marked paths, as the vegetated lava flows conceal deep fissures. There are good views along the valley from beside the abandoned farm buildings at Skógarkot.

5 Svartifoss

Skaftafell's most beautiful feature, Svartifoss ("Black Falls"), is located on an easy hiking trail atop Skaftafell plateau. From the car park near Bölti guesthouse follow the signposts for 10 minutes to the falls that drop into a stunning 30-m- (98-ft-) deep gully (see p25).

6 Ásbyrgi

The top of this huge, curved cliff face makes an excellent vantage point from which to admire the north of Jökulsárgljúfur National Park. From the park headquarters, follow the footpaths for 5 km (3 miles) through woodland to the top of Ásbyrgi (see p24).

7 Heiðmörk Park
MAP Q6

A 28-sq-km (11-sq-mile) spread of lava, woodlands and picnic sites on the edge of Reykjavík city, with easy walking paths looping through it. Extend an excursion here by making a 3-hour circuit of the adjacent lake, Elliðavatn, to view a variety of Iceland's flora.

8 Hveragerði
MAP C5

The steamy hills and valleys immediately north of Hveragerði make for a good half-day hike from town, with hot springs along the way (so bring a towel). There is a marked path but be prepared for boggy ground, a couple of river crossings and unpredictable boiling vents.

Steaming vent, Hveragerði

9 Laugavegur

This stunning 4-day hike runs from Landmannalaugar, past hot springs and obsidian massifs, to the snowbound Hrafntinnusker plateau, then descends steeply to the green valley around Álftavatn. After passing many glacial rivers, a grey gravel desert at the foot of the Mýrdalsjökull icecap and canyons along Markarfljót, the trail ends in the woodland of Þórsmörk (see p30).

10 Þórsmörk
MAP D6 ■ Daily buses from Reykjavík ■ Only accessible mid-Jun–Aug ■ www.thorsmork.is

This beautiful highland valley, with a braided glacial river, is overlooked by Mýrdalsjökull. Carry a map, as few of the many day trails are marked.

TOP 10 ICELANDIC WILD FLOWERS

Moss Campion

1 Mountain Avens (Holtasóley) Iceland's national flower, whose small fleshy leaves and yellow-centred white petals stand about 7 cm (3 in) high.

2 Arctic River Beauty (Eyrarrós) Late-flowering plant with distinctive symmetrical, pointed red petals and long leaves.

3 Moss Campion (Lambagras) Spongy clumps of this bright pink or purple flower brighten up the muddy, shaley slopes.

4 Wild Pansy (Þrenningarfjóla) Beautiful little plant with violet and yellow petals, common locally and abundant in June.

5 Bladder Campion (Holurt) This white flower is found in small spreads, and has a lilac-pink sac behind the petals.

6 Wild Thyme (Blóðberg) Tiny, ground-hugging plant with deep red or purple flowers and distinct thyme scent.

7 Wood Cranesbill (Blágresi) Widespread plant with geranium-like leaves and purple, five-petal flowers; favours woodland edges and reaches 30 cm (12 in) or more.

8 Butterwort (Lyfjagras) Small, solitary plant with hanging blue flowers and cross-shaped leaves at ground level.

9 Northern Green Orchid (Friggjargras) Easily missed in the grass, but look for pointed leaves and little white flowers.

10 Purple Saxifrage (Vetrarblóm) This widespread but very early-flowering, ground-hugging plant has little pink blooms.

🔟 Places for Fine Dining

1 Grillið
MAP J3 ▪ Radisson Blu Saga Hótel, Hagatorg, 107 Reykjavík ▪ 525 9960 ▪ Open 6–10pm Tue–Sat ▪ Ⓚ Ⓚ

This elegant, beautifully furnished rooftop restaurant on the eighth floor of the Radisson Hotel offers some of the best food in Reykjavík. Sous chef Sigurður Helgason was nominated Iceland's chef of the year in 2015. Enjoy an apéritif, and the cityscape, from the Astra Bar.

2 Pakkhús
MAP G5 ▪ Krosseyjarvegi 3, 780 Höfn í Hornafirði ▪ 478 2280 ▪ Open May–Sep: noon–10pm daily ▪ www.pakkhus.is ▪ Ⓚ Ⓚ

In recent years the little harbour town of Höfn in eastern Iceland has become famous for its fresh seafood, especially lobster. This excellent restaurant, housed in an old wooden warehouse down by the water, makes an atmospheric setting for indulging in langoustine. No bookings, so get in early.

3 Gallery
MAP L3 ▪ Hótel Holt, Bergstaðastræti 37, 101 Reykjavík ▪ 552 5700 ▪ Open noon–2pm & 6–9:30pm Tue–Sat ▪ Ⓚ Ⓚ

The island's swankiest restaurant, with a lobby full of fine Icelandic art-works and French-trained chef Friðgeir Eiríksson at the helm. Service is faultless and the menu is based on classic French cuisine: go for the fried monkfish and fennel. Extensive but pricey wine list.

The elegant interior of Gallery

Stylish and innovative Vox

4 Vox
MAP R4 ▪ Hilton Reykjavík Nordica, Suðurlandsbraut 2, 108 Reykjavík ▪ 444 5050 ▪ Open 6:30–10am, 11:30am–2pm & 5:30–10:30pm daily ▪ Ⓚ Ⓚ Ⓚ

This restaurant heads the trend for fresh Icelandic ingredients – delicious seafood straight off the trawlers, game from specialist farms and char fished locally.

5 Grillmarkaðurinn
MAP L2 ▪ Lækjargata 2A, 101 Reykjavík ▪ 571 7777 ▪ Open 11:30am–2pm Mon–Fri, 6–10:30pm Sun–Thu, 6–11:30pm Fri & Sat ▪ Ⓚ Ⓚ

The award-winning chefs here work closely with organic farmers and producers, so the dishes are always fresh, seasonal and delicious. Try the salted cod with lobster salad, Jerusalem artichokes and apples.

6 Rub23
MAP E2 ▪ Kaupvangsstræti 6, 600 Akureyri ▪ 462 2223 ▪ Open 11am–2:30pm & 5pm–late daily ▪ www.rub23.is ▪ Ⓚ Ⓚ

Rub23 serves a decent steak and good seafood, but is best visited for some of the freshest sushi you'll probably ever eat: particularly delicious are the tempura lobster, surimi crab and Arctic char nori maki. There's a takeaway service too.

7 Tjöruhúsið
MAP B2 ▪ Neðstakaupstað, 400 Ísafjörður ▪ 456 4419 ▪ Open noon–2pm & 6:30pm–10pm daily ▪ Ⓚ Ⓚ

There's something very Viking about this long, low barn of a place on

Ísafjörður's waterfront, with diners crowded together on wooden benches, but there is nothing at all rough about its seafood. The rich, creamy soups will warm you through on a cold day, and the portions of pan-fried fish are generous.

(8) Fiskmarkaðurinn

MAP K2 ■ Aðalstræti 12, 101 Reykjavík ■ 578 8877 ■ Open 11:30am–2pm, 6–11:30pm daily ■ ⓀⓀⓀ

"The Fish Market" is Asian and the sushi outstanding. Produce is sourced locally where possible and the tasting menu is great value.

A cod dish at Fiskmarkaðurinn

(9) Sjávargrillið

MAP L3 ■ Skólavörðustíg 14, 101 Reykjavík ■ 571 1100 ■ Open 11am–3pm Mon–Sat, 5–10:30pm Mon–Fri & Sun, 5–11:30pm Sat ■ ⓀⓀ

For excellent seafood right in the city centre, try this cozy candlelit restaurant, offering traditional specialities such as marinated minke whale, puffin and skyr.

(10) Fjöruborðið

MAP C5 ■ Eyrarbraut 3a, 825 Stokkseyri ■ 483 1550 ■ Open Jun–Aug: noon–9pm daily; Sep–May: 4–9pm daily ■ www.fjorubordid.is ■ ⓀⓀ

Famed for its lobster, this restaurant is located in an old timber building in Stokkseyri, an hour's drive from Reykjavík. The rest of the menu features lamb and other local stalwarts. Book in advance.

TOP 10 ICELANDIC FOODS

Roasted Arctic Char

1 Lamb
This is the mainstay of Icelandic cuisine. Lamb is eaten fresh, smoked, turned into sausages, or preserved in whey after pressing.

2 Lobster
Superb and plentiful, best served as tails with butter and, perhaps, a little garlic seasoning or cream.

3 Salmon
Wild-caught Atlantic salmon is firm and rich. It is usually eaten smoked or marinated with herbs and served as butter-soft gravlax.

4 Caviar
Iceland's supplies come from capelin and lumpfish, not the classic sturgeon, but are just as delicious.

5 Cod
Most often snacked on as dried, chewy *harðfiskur*, but also cooked fresh and used in soups.

6 Hákarl
Greenland shark, fermented in sand for 6 months to break down toxins. Eye-wateringly strong.

7 Brennivín
Icelandic vodka, flavoured with caraway seeds and affectionately known as "Black Death". Use sparingly.

8 Skyr
Similar to set yoghurt, available in any supermarket in a range of flavours.

9 Arctic Char
Freshwater fish with a beautifully subtle flavour. The best come from Þingvallavatn and Mývatn.

10 Ptarmigan
Plump, partridge-like bird which takes the place of turkey at traditional Christmas meals in Iceland.

For a key to restaurant price ranges see p81

Cheaper Eats

1 Bæjarins Beztu Pylsur
MAP L2 ■ Tryggvagata, Reykjavík ■ Open 10–1am Sun–Thu, 10am–4:30am Fri & Sat ■ Ⓚ

A Reykjavík institution, this mobile cart can be found parked down near the waterfront and its *pylsur* (hot dogs) are a must for visitors to the city. Your money buys you a bright red sausage in a bun, topped with crispy fried onions, ketchup, mustard and a squirt of remoulade sauce.

2 Café Garðurinn
MAP M2 ■ Klapparstígur 37, Reykjavík ■ 561 2345 ■ Open 11am–6:30pm (to 8:30pm May–Sep) Mon, Tue, Thu & Fri, 11am–5pm Wed, noon–5pm Sat ■ Ⓚ

This small vegetarian café has a set menu that changes weekly. Flavour combinations are inventive and delicious. They offer a range of crepes, flans, stews and pastas, but tasty soups (served with bread) and quiches are their forte. The "dish of the day" is excellent value. They serve great coffee and cakes too.

3 Jómfrúin
MAP L2 ■ Lækjargata 4, Reykjavík ■ 551 0100 ■ Open 11am–6pm daily ■ Ⓚ

Calling this place a Danish sandwich shop does not do it justice: a good

Jómfrúin, Reykjavík

smørrebrød (open sandwich) involves a choice of prawns, herring, smoked lamb, cheese and countless other ingredients, served on a thick slice of heavy rye bread, and Jómfrúin delivers in style. Do include the fried plaice in your selection.

4 Búllan
MAP K1 ■ Geirsgata 1, Reykjavík ■ 511 1888 ■ Open 11:30am–9pm daily ■ Ⓚ

Standing isolated on a corner at the harbour entrance, inside a 1950s concrete shell, this tiny, glass-fronted diner does just one thing – burgers – and does it extremely well. This is a great place if you need a cheap, decent, filling meal after staggering off a whale-watching boat. Be prepared to queue up as it is always busy.

The tiny diner of Búllan

5 Lobster Hut

MAP L2 ■ Corner of Hverfisgata and Lækjargata, Reykjavík ■ 772 1710 ■ Open 11am–7pm daily, except during bad weather ■ ⓚⓚ

One of few options on Reykjavík's street food scene, this food truck serves local *humarsúpa* (lobster soup) and lobster sandwiches. Icelandic "lobster" is actually langoustine, a smaller crustacean whose flavour is extremely close to that of its larger cousin, the rock lobster. The hut's generous portions are grilled fresh to order.

6 T-Bær Café

MAP C5 ■ Strandakirkja ■ 483 3150 ■ Open 10am–10pm Mon–Wed & Fri–Sun, 2–10pm Thurs ■ ⓚ

Tucked away in southern Iceland's three-building hamlet of Strandakirkja, this café is worth seeking out not just for its decent coffee and cakes, but for the beautiful, uninhabited stretch of rocky coastline just over the road – popular with playful seals in the long summer evenings.

7 Krúa Thai

MAP K2 ■ Tryggvagata 14, Reykjavík ■ 561 0039 ■ Open 11:30am–9:30pm Mon–Fri, noon–9:30pm Sat, 5–9:30pm Sun ■ ⓚ

One of the few places left in Iceland where you can get an economical restaurant meal – even if it's only a single course. All the old favourites, from panang curry to *tom kha gai*, are served in a relaxed, fast-food ambience. The beer is not too expensive either.

8 Icelandic Fish & Chips

MAP K2 ■ Tryggvagata 11, Reykjavík ■ 511 1118 ■ Open 11:30am–9pm Mon–Fri, noon–10pm Sat & Sun ■ ⓚ

Up at Reykjavík's old harbour, this tidy organic bistro delivers just what it says: choose from Icelandic cod, plaice, halibut or catfish served with skyronaisse in a variety of flavours and oven-grilled chips. Everything is tasty and well cooked.

9 Þrír Frakkar

MAP L3 ■ Baldursgata 14, Reykjavík ■ 552 3939 ■ Open 11:30am–2:30pm & 6–10pm Mon–Fri, 6–11pm Sat & Sun ■ ⓚⓚ

Set in a charming building in a quiet residential area, the "Three Overcoats" specializes in seafood, with excellent trout, lobster and soups served with a French–Asian twist. The whale steak, pan-fried guillemot breast, smoked puffin and horse tenderloin are cooked in traditional Icelandic style.

Pan-fried salted cod, Þrír Frakkar

10 Hótel Bláfell

MAP H4 ■ Bláfell, Breiðdalsvík ■ 475 6625 ■ Open 10am–8pm daily ■ ⓚⓚ

This cozy café is a great place for a light lunch on the long drive between the East Fjords and Höfn. The tall windows provide a broad view of the coast, and the cakes are gorgeous.

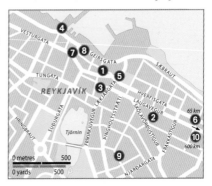

For a key to restaurant price ranges see p81

🔟 Bars, Clubs and Cafés

① Austur Steikhús
MAP L2 ▪ Austurstræti 7, 101 Reykjavík ▪ 568 1907 ▪ Open 8pm–1am Thu, 8pm–4:30am Fri & Sat

This well known club – popular among both tourists and locals – boasts a trendy clientele (including celebrities and media people) and an exclusive VIP area offering table service. Live DJs play long into the night and keep the dance floor busy. There's also an extensive menu of wines, cocktails, beers and shots available at the bar.

Austur Steikhús

② B5
MAP L2 ▪ Bankastræti 5, 101 Reykjavík ▪ 552 9600 ▪ Open 11am–midnight Sun–Wed, 10:30am–1am Thu, 10:30am–2am Fri & Sat

A multifunctional venue, B5 is a laid-back café by day (with a proper library), which transforms into a popular bar-club after dark. If you are planning a party it has two private lounges (one built in an old bank vault) available for hire.

③ Lebowski Bar
MAP M2 ▪ Laugavegur 20a, 101 Reykjavík ▪ 552 2300 ▪ Open 11:30am–1am Sun–Thu, until 4am Fri & Sat ▪ www.lebowski.is

Fans of the movie *The Big Lebowski* will appreciate this quirky bowling-themed bar, with its delicious burgers and 18 variations on the White Russian cocktail. Play "spin the wheel" for free drinks. DJs play every night, bands play at weekends and a big screen shows live sport.

Micro Bar, Reykjavík

④ Micro Bar
MAP L2 ▪ Austurstræti 6, 101 Reykjavík ▪ 847 9084 ▪ Open 4pm–midnight daily

Blink and you'll miss this hole in the wall at the back of the City Center Hotel. Choose from 250 different craft beers, ales, stouts and lagers, including brews you won't find anywhere else in Iceland. It's run by the folks behind the Gæðingur micro-brewery in the north of the country.

⑤ Bjarni Fel
MAP L2 ▪ Austurstræti 20, 101 Reykjavík ▪ 561 2240 ▪ Open 9am–1am Sun–Thu, 10am–4:30am Fri & Sat

Locals love this sports bar, named after Icelandic football legend and sports commentator Bjarni Felixson. Enjoy the views on multiple TV screens as you sample a good selection of pub food and cold beer.

⑥ Prikið
MAP L2 ▪ Bankastræti 12, 101 Reykjavík ▪ 551 2866 ▪ Open 8am–1am Mon–Thu, 11am–4:30am Fri & Sat, noon–1am Sun ▪ www.prikid.is

A 50s-style diner as well as a nightclub, Prikið offers classics such

Prikið's classic diner-style food

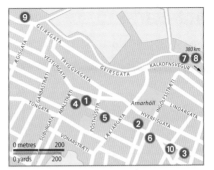

as milkshakes, American pancakes and chicken burritos. During the day it is the perfect spot for people-watching thanks to its location on the city's main shopping thoroughfare, while at night it transforms into a lively and fun hip-hop hang-out with DJs, live music and a packed dance floor (see p80).

7 Götubarinn
MAP E2 ■ Hafnarstræti 95–96, 600 Akureyri ■ 462 4747 ■ Open 5pm–1am Thu, 8pm–4am Fri & Sat; summer: 5pm–4am Fri & Sat

This charming bar in the centre of Akureyri boasts an excellent selection of beers. Its unique interior design, including old street signs, pays homage to Akureyri's history. This is a popular choice for a night out in the city.

8 Café Amour
MAP E2 ■ Ráðhústorg 9, Akureyri ■ 461 3030 ■ Open 11am–1am Sun–Thu (4am Fri & Sat)

Set right on the "circle", Akureyri's downtown square, Café Amour is about the only café outside of Reykjavík that can really claim to have a touch of the city's chic ambience. It is a great place to hang out over a coffee during the day, making use of the outdoor seating and watching the crowds. After dark, come for a beer, occasional live bands or simply to watch major sports events on TV.

9 Slippbarinn
MAP K1 ■ Mýrargata 2, 101 Reykjavík ■ 560 8080 ■ Open 11:30am–midnight Sun–Wed (1am Thu–Sat) ■ www.slippbarinn.is

The impressive cocktail menu offered at this bar changes regularly, but the harbour views remain consistently inspiring. Located in the Icelandair Hotel Reykjavík Marina, Slippbarinn hosts Icelandic live music, as well as art shows and

"pop-up" events of all sorts. Brunch is served at weekends and happy hour is from 3 to 6pm every day.

10 Kaffibarinn
MAP L3 ■ Bergstaðastræti 1, 101 Reykjavík ■ 551 1588 ■ Open 3pm–1am Mon–Fri, 3pm–4:30am Sat & Sun ■ www.kaffibarinn.is

The red corrugated iron exterior, just off Reykjavík's main shopping area, conceals Kaffibarinn's dark interior, with its table-top candles and arty magazines. A trendy and popular place to meet for the first beer of the evening, there are DJs every night and, on occasion, live bands.

Kaffibarinn's distinctive exterior

🔟 Iceland for Free

Aurora borealis over Jökulsárlón

1 Aurora Borealis

Extremely low light pollution in its night skies makes Iceland a superlative place to see the dancing curtains of the northern lights. Come in winter (they do not appear on short summer nights) during years in which there is increased solar activity, and get away from Reykjavík for the best views *(see p59)*.

2 Camping

Most people make use of Iceland's inexpensive camp sites, but it is possible to camp anywhere for free outside of the city boundaries or national parks. Always ask for permission from local landowners, as they can suggest the best places to pitch a tent away from livestock or crops. Leave things as you find them, taking your rubbish away with you.

3 Berjamór

Join Icelanders in picking wild crowberries (similar to blueberries) from late summer to early autumn. They grow all over the place, but ask around to find the best spots. Don't be greedy: leave some for the birds, who need them to get through the harsh winters.

4 Natural Thermal Pools

Since Viking times, hot springs have been channelled into fabulous natural spas. The pick of the bunch is at Landmannalaugar *(see pp30–31)*, but others include Seljavallalaug *(see p112)* near Skógar, right below the site of the 2010 eruption that closed down European airspace, and Grjótagjá *(see p97)* at Mývatn, though this one is usually too hot to enter.

Reykjavík as seen from Perlan

5 Views from Perlan in Reykjavík
MAP M6

The capital's most visible landmark *(see p77)* sits relatively high on wooded Öskjuhlíð hill, with a 360° panorama of the city and nearby coast – on clear days you can look across the sea to the icy cone at the tip of the Snæfellsjökull volcano.

6 Wildlife Watching

Iceland makes a great place to spy on wildlife. You will find seals and teeming seabird colonies all around the coast (especially at Vík, Látrabjarg and the Westman Islands), reindeer herds in the eastern highlands, shy Arctic foxes everywhere, and rare ducks and other waterfowl at Mývatn lake.

7 Þingvellir Parliament Site

MAP C5

Even if it weren't intimately linked to key events in Icelandic history, Þingvellir (see pp12–13) would still be a spectacular place: a broad rift valley sided in basalt columns where the Eurasian and American continental plates are visibly tearing apart. There's some good hiking here too.

8 Scale Model of Iceland at the Ráðhúsið

MAP K2 ▪ Tjarnargata 11, Reykjavík ▪ 411 1111 ▪ Open 8am–7pm Mon–Fri, noon–6pm Sat & Sun

Plan or relive your travels with this enormous 3-D relief map of Iceland, complete with clearly marked glaciers, volcanoes and fjords. Finish up by feeding the ducks and swans outside at Tjörnin lake.

9 Spectacular Waterfalls

Meltwater from Europe's largest glaciers feeds some mighty waterfalls, where you can lose yourself in the noise and spray. The closest to Reykjavík are Gullfoss (see pp18–19) and Skógafoss (see p45), but it's worth the effort to reach Dynjandi (see p45) in the Westfjords and Dettifoss (see p44), Europe's largest waterfall, in the north.

10 Smoking Lava Fields

Get a taste of what the ongoing eruption at Holuhraun is like by hiking out to the still-smoking scenes of similar recent events at Krafla (see p21) and Fimmvörðuháls (see p60), site of the 2010 eruption.

Smoking lava fields, Krafla

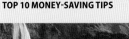

TOP 10 MONEY-SAVING TIPS

Camping by Seljalandsfoss

1 Take advantage of online discounts from Icelandair, WOW Air or easyJet.
www.icelandair.co.uk
www.wowair.co.uk
www.easyjet.co.uk

2 Visit off-season (October–June). Some sights are closed or inaccessible, but accommodation and car-rental costs drop significantly.

3 If self-catering, bring in your duty-free limit of alcohol and food.

4 Bus passes limit you to specific routes and timetables, but are cheaper than buying individual tickets.

5 A Hostelling International (YHA) card scores discounts at Iceland's many official youth hostels.
www.hihostels.com

6 Carry a tent. Iceland's many camp sites are usually well equipped and cost a fraction of a hotel bed.

7 Bring a sleeping bag with you to capitalize on guesthouses' lower "sleeping bag" room rates.

8 Enjoy an inexpensive swim, sauna or hot tub session at public swimming pools around the country.

9 You can cycle around Iceland in a month, making savings on transport.

10 Buy locally produced smoked salmon, woollen jumpers or outdoor gear – still costly, but excellent value. Don't forget to claim tax refunds for items over ISK 4,000 (see p125).

🔟 Festivals

Menningarnótt fireworks

① Menningarnótt
www.menningarnott.is

One night in August is designated Culture Night, during which downtown Reykjavík is closed to traffic as stages are set up, performers throng the streets and fireworks light up the night sky over the city. The entertainment is mainly amateur, but well-known groups also participate at times.

② Reykjavík International Film Festival (RIFF)
www.riff.is

A selection of the year's best world cinema gets a screening at the Reykjavík International Film Festival in late September, with events all around town. The festival includes an Icelandic Panorama Section as well as side events like Swim-in Cinema, Film Concert and masterclasses with film-makers.

③ Reykjavík Arts Festival
www.artfest.is

This annual showcase of concerts, opera, dance and theatre has been held in mid-May since 1970. For three weeks every year it brings together major cultural venues and unconventional spaces throughout the city.

④ Djasshátíð – Reykjavík Jazz Festival
www.reykjavikjazz.is

The latest in jazz and blues comes to Reykjavík in August. There is always a smattering of international stars but the surprise is the quality and abundance of local talent. Do not miss the "Guitar Party" event.

⑤ Fiskidagurinn Mikli
MAP E2 ■ www.fiskidagurinnmikli.is

Early August (always the first or second Saturday of the month) sees Dalvík, a nondescript fishing village near Akureyri, draw the crowds with its "Fish Soup Day", a sort of eccentric, friendly social event for which Iceland should be famous.

Street theatre at the Reykjavík Arts Festival

Apart from outdoor seafood buffets, look for homes displaying flaming torches – a sign that free fish soup is available.

6 Myrkir Músíkdagar

Held in February during odd-numbered years, the "Dark Music Days" festival brightens up Reykjavík's winter gloom with workshops and almost exclusively Icelandic contemporary music performances, ranging from avant-garde to opera.

7 Reykjavík Pride
www.reykjavikpride.com

Held annually since 1999, Reykjavík's Gay Pride festival goes from strength to strength, though the August timetable is asking a bit from the weather and rain is not unknown during the Saturday parade, which starts at the BSÍ bus terminal and winds through downtown Reykjavík.

8 Þjóðhátíð Vestmannaeyjar
www.dalurinn.is

Westman Islands Festival is not for the faint-hearted: camping for 4 days in August in a sodden volcano crater, serenaded by an unending line-up of Icelandic rock at maximum decibels and getting drunk enough to try skinny-dipping in the sea along with thousands of others.

9 Kirkjubæjarklaustur Chamber Music Festival
MAP E5 ■ www.kammertonleikar.is

This annual summer festival showcases international talent and is set among south Iceland's largest lava fields. It is also a chance to explore small-town Iceland.

10 Síldarævintýri
MAP D2

Every summer the small north-coast town of Siglufjörður, once the North Atlantic's busiest herring port, holds a music festival known as the Herring Adventure in honour of the fish. It includes everything from traditional folk singing to Sigur Rós.

TOP 10 ICELANDIC MUSICIANS

Björk in concert

1 Björk
This singer is Iceland's best-known musical export, though nowhere near as popular at home as abroad.

2 Sigur Rós
The "post-rock" band Sigur Rós blends elements of pop, classical and folk music, and has unique vocals.

3 KK
Folk guitarist Kristján Kristjánsson is the Arlo Guthrie of Iceland, quite often teaming up with the veteran musician Magnús Eiríksson.

4 Stefán Íslandi
Born in 1907, Stefán Íslandi performed as an opera tenor in the US until his death in 1994.

5 Sigrún Hjálmtýsdóttir
A leading opera soprano and jazz singer, Sigrún Hjálmtýsdóttir has performed with José Carreras and Placido Domingo.

6 Kristinn Sigmundsson
Massive operatic bass, Sigmundsson one of iceland's best known international opera singers.

7 Mugison
Iceland's version of fusion-delta blues, a slide guitarist from the Westfjords, Mugison, has an astounding voice.

8 Emiliana Torrini
Part Icelandic, part Italian, sweet-voiced singer Torrini is the first Icelander to top the German charts.

9 Bubbi Morthens
Bubbi Morthens is a mix of punk, Bruce Springsteen and Johnny Cash (minus the hair).

10 Kristinn Árnason
A brilliant classical guitarist, Kristinn Árnason also effortlessly manages the crossover into rock.

Iceland
Area by Area

Multicoloured volcanic landscape,
Landmannalaugar, South Iceland

ⓑ Reykjavík

Statue, National Museum

The Reykjavík area covers the city centre, plus a handful of satellite suburbs. The city's tiny core consists of a historic precinct of lanes near the old harbour, easily covered on foot in a day. While the municipal buildings are made of stone or concrete – practical protection against the fierce winter winds – most of the area is residential, comprising old wooden houses, weatherproofed in brightly coloured corrugated iron. Here you will find most of the shops, cafés, restaurants and nightclubs, alongside museums and galleries. A distinctive landmark is Öskjuhlið hill, with panoramic views of more distant sights and suburbs.

AREA MAP OF REYKJAVÍK

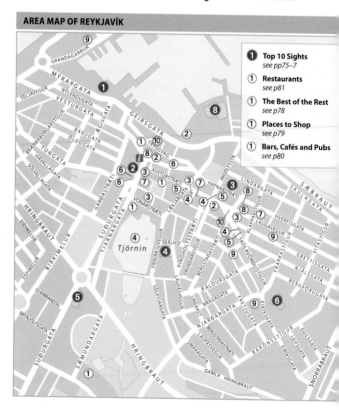

1 Top 10 Sights
see pp75–7

1 Restaurants
see p81

1 The Best of the Rest
see p78

1 Places to Shop
see p79

1 Bars, Cafés and Pubs
see p80

1 Historic Midtown and Harbour

MAP K1

The midtown is the site of Iceland's first Viking settlement and the city's oldest building (on Lækjatorg Square). A statue of Jón Sigurðsson *(see p37)* faces the 1881 Parliament House, which replaced the Alþing's home at Þingvellir. Visit the old harbour, Saga Museum and whaling fleet.

Historic buildings, midtown Reykjavík

2 Landnámssýningin (Settlement Exhibition)

MAP K2 ■ Aðalstræti 16 ■ 411 6370 ■ Open 10am–5pm daily ■ Adm ■ www.reykjavik871.is

This impressive exhibition comprises the in-situ remains of a large Viking-age longhouse, possibly belonging to Iceland's first settler, Norwegian Ingólfur Arnarson, who sailed to Iceland around AD 870. There are virtually no other contemporary remains in such good condition. Its location under the capital's streets makes it even more incredible.

3 Safnahúsið (Culture House)

MAP L2 ■ Hverfisgata 15 ■ 545 1400 ■ Open 11am–5pm daily ■ Adm (Wed free) ■ On-site café at weekends ■ Guided tours available ■ www.thjodmenning.is

Iceland's medieval manuscripts were returned in the 1970s after centuries in Denmark and are now displayed in the old National Library. There is also an excellent account of their composition and history.

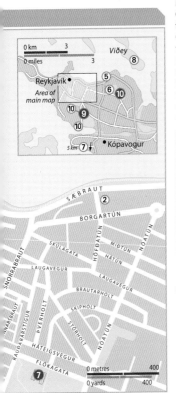

Medieval manuscript, Safnahúsið

4 Listasafn Íslands (National Gallery)

MAP L3 ■ Fríkirkjuvegur 7 ■ 515 9600 ■ Open 10am–5pm Tue–Sun ■ www.listasafn.is

The nation's main collection of art, housed in a former warehouse, concentrates on early 20th-century Icelandic painters. The estimated 10,000 works are continually rotated.

5 Þjóðminjasafn Íslands
(National Museum)

MAP K3 ▪ Suðurgata 41 ▪ 530 2200 ▪
Open May–mid-Sep: 10am–5pm
daily; mid-Sep–Apr: 11am–5pm Tue–
Sun ▪ Adm ▪ www.thjodmin
jasafn.is

Documenting Iceland's history and culture from the earliest evidence of settlement to the present, the museum offers interactive learning opportunities for visitors. Whether it is Viking grave goods, medieval statues or Björk's musical career, there is something for everyone in this interesting exhibition covering the museum's two floors.

6 Hallgrímskirkja

MAP M3 ▪ Skólavörðuholti ▪
510 1000 ▪ Open 9am–5pm daily ▪
Cathedral free; tower adm ▪
www.hallgrimskirkja.is

The largest in Iceland, this 74-m- (240-ft-) high church took 40 years to build and resembles a volcanic formation, covered in hexagonal pillars. The sound of the stunning church organ, fitted with 5,275 pipes, is a highlight. Take the lift to the tower for views over Reykjavík's colourful rooftops and Leifur Eiríksson's statue.

Leifur Eiríksson

THE SETTLEMENT OF REYKJAVÍK

When Ingólfur Arnarson first saw Iceland on his voyage from Norway in AD 870, he threw overboard his valuable wooden seat-posts and vowed to settle wherever they washed up. They were finally found in a broad, fertile, steamy inlet on the island's southwest, which Ingólfur named Reykjavík ("Smoky Bay").

7 Kjarvalsstaðir
(Reykjavík Art Museum)

MAP N4 ▪ Flókagata 24 ▪ 517 1290 ▪
Open 10am–5pm daily ▪ Guided tours by arrangement ▪ Adm ▪ www.
listasafnreykjavikur.is

Jóhannes Kjarval (1885–1972), born in a tiny village in the northeast, studied painting in Europe. On returning to Iceland he began incorporating the landscapes into his brightly coloured paintings. Though considered Iceland's greatest artist, his work often controversially blended folklore, Christianity and paganism. Apart from his works, this museum also exhibits contemporary Icelandic and foreign art.

8 Harpa

MAP L2 ▪ Austurstræti 17 ▪
528 5000 ▪ Guided tours year-round
▪ www.harpa.is

Harpa – the Reykjavík Concert Hall and Conference Centre – is the most important classical and performance

Harpa, Reykjavík's Concert Hall and Conference Centre

venue in the country, home to the Iceland Symphony Orchestra and the Icelandic Opera. With a façade by renowned artist Olafur Eliasson, it is a symbol of the revitalization of Reykjavík's historic waterfront and of Iceland's renewed dynamism.

Perlan's mirrored-glass dome

⑨ Perlan
MAP M6 ▪ Öskjuhlíð ▪ Bus 18 from Hlemmur ▪ Building entry free ▪ www.perlan.is

Just south of the city centre, wooded Öskjuhlíð hill is covered in a network of walking and cycling tracks, some of which are surprisingly secluded. The summit is capped by the mirrored-glass dome of Perlan ("the Pearl"). This imaginative building, made from converted cylindrical water tanks, has fabulous city panoramas from the outside viewing deck. Inside, there's a renowned revolving restaurant (see p81), and a central atrium full of tropical palms.

⑩ Laugardalur Park and Recreation Area
MAP R4 ▪ Laugardalur ▪ Bus 14 from Hlemmur ▪ Pool: 411 5100 ▪ Open Apr–Aug: 6:30am–10pm Mon–Fri, 8am–10pm Sat & Sun ▪ Park free; activities adm

East of the city centre, Laugardalur Park is a great spot to join local families relaxing. The Botanic Gardens have a zoo full of native species and a duck pond. You can skate in winter at the adjacent sports centre. The naturally heated 50-m- (164-ft-) long outdoor pool, with three smaller play pools and hot tubs, is open year-round.

A DAY IN REYKJAVÍK

▶ MORNING

Kick off the day the way many Icelanders do – by having a swim at the central **Sundhöllin** indoor pool. After a coffee at **Kaffitár** on Bankastræti, head for the **National Museum** and get a solid grounding in Icelandic history, though don't burn out by trying to cover it all on a single trip. Amble down to get some fresh air and feed the birds at **Tjörnin** (see p78), before ducking inside **City Hall** for a look at the giant relief map of the country, or to catch a lunchtime concert. Sit out on the grass at **Austurvöllur Square** to admire the humble Reykjavík Cathedral, the Art Deco Hótel Borg and the Parliament House. Then spend half an hour among Viking remains at the excellent **Settlement Exhibition** (see p75), which is located nearby.

AFTERNOON

Reboot your energy levels with a bowl of lamb soup at **Café Paris** (see p80), then shop for jewellery, clothes or souvenirs along **Laugavegur**. Head uphill, past a street of colourful houses on Klapparstígur, to take in the cityscape from the top of **Hallgrímskirkja** (see p76). If you have room for another museum, soak up some Saga-Age ambience at the **Culture House** (see p75). Walk north to **Harpa** to take in a concert, or to see the striking **Solar Voyager** sculpture and historic **Höfði House** (see p78). Plan an assault of the city's nightclubs – **Prikið** (see p66), in the city centre, is the best place to start.

See map on pp74–5

The Best of the Rest

① Norræna Húsið
MAP K4 ▪ Sturlugata 5 ▪ 551 7030 ▪ Open daily; library: Jun–Aug 10am–5pm; Sep–May noon–5pm; exhibition room: Tue–Sun noon–5pm ▪ www.nordice.is

Exhibitions, concerts and a library devoted to Nordic culture.

Höfði House

② Höfði House
MAP P2 ▪ Borgartún

In this simple, whitewashed house, Mikhail Gorbachev and Ronald Reagan ended the Cold War in 1986. Nearby sculpture *Solar Voyager* honours Viking travels.

③ Alþingishúsið
MAP L2 ▪ Austurvöllur ▪ 563 0500 ▪ Check for opening times ▪ www.althingi.is

This building houses the national parliament. Founded at Þingvellir in AD 930, it relocated here in 1881.

Viðey seabird

④ Tjörnin
MAP K3

Locals bring their children to feed the ducks, geese and swans at this stone-edged lake in the city centre.

⑤ Sigurjón Ólafsson Sculpture Museum
MAP Q1 ▪ Laugarnestangi 70 ▪ Buses 12 & 15 ▪ 553 2906 ▪ Open Jun–Aug: 2–5pm Tue–Sun; Sep–May: 2–5pm Sat & Sun ▪ www.lso.is

Once the studio of Sigurjón Ólafsson, this building displays his sculptures and hosts summer concerts.

⑥ Ásmundur Sveinsson Sculpture Museum
MAP Q4 ▪ Sigtún ▪ 553 2155 ▪ Open May–Sep: 10am–5pm daily; Oct–Apr: 1–5pm daily ▪ Adm

With its Mediterranean and African influences, this building is as interesting as the displayed works of the renowned sculptor.

⑦ Hafnarfjörður
MAP P6 ▪ Bus 1 from Hamraborg ▪ www.hafnarfjordur.is, www.fjorukrain.is

This seaside suburb of Reykjavík is home to good restaurants and an annual Viking festival.

⑧ Viðey
MAP P5 ▪ mid-May–Sep: 8 ferries daily from Skarfabakka, and 2 daily from Reykjavík's Old Harbour and Harpa ▪ www.videy.com

Just off Reykjavík, this grassy isle boasts Iceland's oldest stone building (now a restaurant), thousands of seabirds and the Imagine Peace Tower.

⑨ The Einar Jónsson Sculpture Museum
MAP M3 ▪ Eiríksgata ▪ 561 3797 ▪ Open Jun–mid-Sep: 1–5pm Tue–Sun; mid-Sep–Nov, Feb–May: 1–5pm Sat & Sun ▪ Adm ▪ www.lej.is

Iceland's first modern sculptor, Einar Jónsson's (1874–1954) 300 plaster and bronze statues are on display.

⑩ Nauthólsvík Geothermal Beach
MAP M6 ▪ Changing rooms open mid-May–mid Aug 11am–1pm Mon–Fri (and 5pm–7pm Mon & Wed), 11am–3pm Sat

This yellow-sand beach is set right on the waterfront south of the city centre, complete with open-air hot tubs and pool. No less fun for being entirely artificial, its geothermal pumps keep the water at 18°C.

Places to Shop

1 Kirsuberjatréð
MAP L2 ■ Vesturgata 4 ■
562 8990 ■ www.kirs.is
This unique store, run by a women's cooperative, offers distinctly Icelandic garments, fish-skin accessories, glassware, jewellery and gifts.

2 The Viking
MAP L2 ■ Laugavegur 1
■ 551 1250
Known for its friendly service and long opening hours, this gift shop has been in the same family for over 50 years. Now a chain with five stores across Iceland.

3 Thorvaldsens Bazar
MAP L2 ■ Austurstræti 4 ■
551 3509 ■ www.thorvaldsens.is
This charity shop has been in business for over a century and specializes in handmade Icelandic goods – knitted jumpers, local woodcarvings and silver jewellery.

4 Eymundsson
MAP L3 ■ Skólavörðustíg 11 ■
540 2350
This excellent bookshop offers a wide range of maps, from road atlases to detailed hiking maps, as well as English-language books on Iceland, stationery and T-shirts. There is also a good café.

5 12 Tónar
MAP L3 ■ Skólavörðustíg 15 ■
511 5656
Selling music CDs and vinyl, this shop also hosts concerts (especially during the summer) by an eclectic inventory of local artists covering jazz, classical and pop.

6 Kraum
MAP L2 ■ Aðalstræti 10 ■
517 7797 ■ www.kraum.is
Local designers display and sell their clothes and accessories here. Look out for attractive silver and black lava jewellery.

Paper bowls at Kirsuberjatréð

7 Aurum
MAP L2 ■ Banankstræti 4 ■
551 2770 ■ www.aurum.is
The jewellery of Guðbjörg Kristín Ingvarsdóttir is modelled on the landscape and flora of Iceland, using precious metals to create delicate, fluid designs that are both modern and timeless.

8 Michelsen Watchmakers
MAP L2 ■ Laugavegur 15 ■
511 1900
Great old-style watchmaker, with a workshop full of half-repaired pre-digital timepieces. Sells Rolexes and other classic wristwatches.

9 Búríð – The Icelandic Pantry
MAP K1 ■ Grandagarður 35 ■ 551 8400 ■ blog.burid.is
Located in the old fishermen's huts by the harbour, this gourmet shop offers a tempting selection of cheeses and local specialities such as birch syrup.

10 Kolaportið Flea Market
MAP L2 ■ Tryggvagata 19 ■ 562 5030 ■ Open 11am–5pm Sat & Sun
Join the locals in spending a couple of hours sifting through acres of household junk at this market and you might uncover unexpectedly stylish designer clothing. Good home-grown vegetables, too.

See map on pp74–5

Bars, Cafés and Pubs

Café Paris

① Café Paris
MAP L2 ▪ Austurstræti 14 ▪ 551 1020 ▪ Open Jun–Aug 8am–1am daily; Sep–May 9am–1am daily

Try the sandwiches for lunch at this café, popular with locals and tourists alike. Sit outside in good weather to enhance the Parisian ambience.

② Prikið
MAP L2 ▪ Bankastræti 12 ▪ 551 2866

This friendly café-diner, frequented by an arty crowd, has a bar feel by night. There are hip-hop DJs at weekends (see p66).

③ Vegamót
MAP L3 ▪ Vegamótstígur 4 ▪ 511 3040

A restaurant-bar with a great patio, Vegamót is busy at lunchtime and after office hours. People-watch over a drink, or sample the Mediterranean menu.

④ Íslenski Barinn
MAP L2 ▪ Ingólfsstræti 1a ▪ 517 6767

Traditional Icelandic delicacies and beer are served here. There are pancakes and coffee every Sunday. Live music is hosted on Thursdays, Fridays and Sundays.

⑤ Grái Kötturinn
MAP L2 ▪ Hverfisgata 16a ▪ 551 1544 ▪ Open 7:15am–3pm Mon–Fri, 8am–3pm Sat & Sun

Huge breakfasts are served at this trendy basement café. It's also a popular place to get coffee after a night out.

⑥ Hornið
MAP L2 ▪ Hafnarstræti 15 ▪ 551 3340

In business since 1979, this family-run, cozy Italian pizzeria was one of the first places to serve espresso in Iceland. Their fresh seafood pastas are superb.

⑦ Café Rosenberg
MAP M3 ▪ Klapparstígur 25 ▪ 551 2442

A classic folk, jazz and blues bar, this venue also serves simple meals. Although the original building burned down in 2007, the venue has been open for decades.

⑧ Celtic Cross
MAP L2 ▪ Hverfisgata 26 ▪ 571 1033

Crowds pile into this popular Irish bar, where soups, breads and an exceptional vibe are all on the menu.

⑨ Sandholt
MAP M3 ▪ Laugavegur 36 ▪ 551 3524

Tasty breads, Danish pastries, quiches, chocolates, sandwiches and superb coffee are all served at this family-run bakery.

⑩ Mokka
MAP L3 ▪ Skólavörðustíg 3a ▪ 552 1174

Said to be the capital's oldest café (it opened in 1958), the no-frills Mokka is credited with spearheading caffeine culture in Iceland.

Restaurants

Interior of Við Tjörnina

1 Við Tjörnina
MAP K2 ▪ Tjarnargata 11 ▪ 551 8666 ▪ www.vidtjornina.is ▪ Ⓚ Ⓚ

At this smart restaurant overlooking Tjörnin, with house speciality seafood dishes, customers can get a free bag of bread to feed the ducks.

2 Kolabrautin
MAP L2 ▪ Austurbakki 1 ▪ 519 9700 ▪ Kitchen: 5:30–10:30pm daily; bar: 4pm–midnight daily ▪ Ⓚ Ⓚ

Enjoy classic Italian cuisine made with Icelandic produce and innovative cocktails (happy hour is 4–6pm daily), with the best panoramic view of Reykjavík.

3 Lækjarbrekka
MAP L2 ▪ Bankastræti 2 ▪ 551 4430 ▪ Open 11:30am–10pm daily ▪ Ⓚ Ⓚ Ⓚ

Housed in an old storehouse in the city centre, this famous eatery is full of period furnishings. It serves top-notch traditional seafood.

4 Torfan
MAP L2 ▪ Amtmannstíg 1 ▪ 561 3303 ▪ www.torfan.is ▪ Ⓚ Ⓚ

This intimate restaurant serves classic French cuisine with a refreshing Nordic twist.

5 Caruso
MAP L2 ▪ Austurstræti 22 ▪ 562 7335 ▪ Ⓚ Ⓚ

With period decor and an Italian menu, Caruso is elegant but not too formal. Live music at weekends.

6 Fjalakötturinn
MAP K2 ▪ Hótel Reykjavík, Aðalstræti 16 ▪ 514 6060 ▪ Ⓚ Ⓚ

This is a well established restaurant offers delicious, locally inspired dishes including home-grown lamb and salmon. A Viking longhouse was excavated here.

7 Einar Ben
MAP K2 ▪ Veltusund 1 ▪ 511 5090 ▪ Ⓚ Ⓚ Ⓚ

Although there are limited options on the menu (fish, beef or lamb), there's a good chance you will enjoy your best meal in Iceland at this traditional restaurant.

8 Restaurant Reykjavík
MAP K2 ▪ Vesturgata 2 ▪ 552 3030 ▪ Ⓚ Ⓚ

Known for its seafood, this beautiful old wooden warehouse overlooks Ingólfstorg square. Try the delicious seafood buffet.

9 Brauðbær
MAP L3 ▪ Hótel Oðinsvé, Þórsgata 1 ▪ 552 0490 ▪ Ⓚ Ⓚ

Enjoy tasty steaks, burgers, club sandwiches and cold *snorrabrauð* dishes here. There is also a kids' menu available.

10 Perlan
MAP M6 ▪ Öskjuhlíð, 125 Reykjavík ▪ 562 0200 ▪ Open 6:30–10:30pm daily ▪ Ⓚ Ⓚ

This revolving restaurant under a glass dome has fantastic vistas over the city. Service is excellent and the food good, if not always as outstanding as the location. The grilled lamb fillet is reliable, as are the venison dishes.

PRICE CATEGORIES

For a three-course meal for one with half a bottle of wine (or equivalent meal), including taxes and extra charges.

Ⓚ under ISK5,000   Ⓚ Ⓚ ISK5,000–9,000
Ⓚ Ⓚ Ⓚ over ISK9,000

See map on pp74–5

📖 West Iceland and the Snæfellsnes Peninsula

Heading north from Reykjavík, the highway follows the western coastline, famous for its stormy weather. Beyond Hvalfjörður and the exceptional Glymur falls are Akranes and Borgarnes, once home to the notorious Viking Egill Skallagrímsson. The 13th-century historian Snorri Sturluson lived (and was murdered) just inland at Reykholt, close to attractive waterfalls and more saga lore around Laxárdalur. Northwest of Borgarnes, the Snæfellsnes peninsula is dotted with fishing villages and its tip graced by Snæfellsjökull, the conical icecap covering a dormant volcano.

Búðir church

AREA MAP OF WEST ICELAND AND THE SNÆFELLSNES PENINSULA

① Borgarnes Settlement Center

MAP B4 ■ Brákarbraut 13–15, Borgarnes ■ 437 1600 ■ Daily buses from Reykjavík to Borgarnes ■ Open 10am–9pm daily ■ Adm ■ www.landnam.is

These exhibitions explore the Saga of the Settlement Period (AD 870–930) of Iceland, which began with Viking settlers and ended when all free land was taken. A section celebrates Iceland's most famous viking and first poet Egill Skallagrímsson.

② Hraunfossar, Barnafoss and Kaldidalur

MAP C4

About 15 km (9 miles) east up the valley from Reykholt on Route 518, the waterfalls at Hraunfossar and Barnafoss – one gentle, the other violent – are worth a stop en route to Kaldidalur, a stark valley between the icy Ok and Þórisjökull peaks. The road is unsealed, but open in summer to ordinary vehicles (check conditions at www.vegagerdin.is).

Hraunfossar and Barnafoss waterfalls

③ Reykholt

MAP C4 ■ Snorrastofa, Reykholt ■ 433 8000 ■ Open May–Sep: 10am–6pm daily; Oct–Apr: 10am–5pm Mon–Fri; also open by request ■ Adm ■ www.snorrastofa.is

The tiny hamlet of Reykholt belies its importance as the home of Snorri Sturluson (1179–1241), the historian who became tangled in Norway's bid to annex Iceland. Murdered by a rival with the support of the Norwegian king Hákon (he was trapped as he fled down a tunnel beneath his farmhouse), his tale is told at the cultural and medieval centre Snorrastofa. His thermal bathing pool and the restored remains of the tunnel are located nearby.

④ Stykkishólmur

MAP B3 ■ www.stykkisholmur.is ■ Norska Húsið: 438 1640; open Jun–Aug: 11am–5pm daily; Adm; www.norskahusid.is ■ Library of Water: open Jun–Aug: 1–6pm daily; May & Sep: Sat & Sun; Adm; www.libraryofwater.is

This town's wooden buildings recall its 19th-century port heyday, the best being Norska Húsið (Norwegian House). The nearby countryside is dotted with sites from *Eyrbyggja Saga* (see p86). The Library of Water has 24 glass columns filled with water from Iceland's major glaciers.

Hvammstangi

Brú

Norðurá

Vatnsdalur

Arnarvatnsheiði

35

⑥
② Hraunfossar and Barnafoss
⑤ Húsafell

Langjökull

Ok △
90 m

② Kaldidalur

Skorradalsvatn

ugarvatn

ngvallavatn

❶ **Top 10 Sights** *see pp83–5*	
① **Places to Eat** *see p87*	
① **The Best of the Rest** *see p86*	

Snæfellsjökull, the icecapped volcano at the centre of the national park

5 Breiðafjörður and Flatey
MAP B3

Breiðafjörður – the huge, wide bay separating the Snæfellsnes peninsula from the Westfjords to the north – is thick with islands and rocky reefs, providing an ideal breeding ground for marine birds. From Stykkishólmur, you can explore the bay on a tour with Sæferðir (www.seatours.is), or go to Brjánslækur in the Westfjords via Breiðafjörður's largest island, Flatey, once home to an important monastery. For a taste of island life and bird-watching, stay in Flatey's tiny village (www.hotelflatey.is).

6 Búðir
MAP A4

Búðir is a minute place on the south coast of Snæfellsnes, with just a church and a hotel. One can enjoy beautiful seascapes and views of Snæfellsjökull from here. The dark wooden church dates from 1703. Its graveyard and boundaries are encroached upon by the Búðahraun lava field, which is said to be inhabited by creatures from local folklore. Despite its remote location, the romantic Hótel Búðir (see p130) is famous for being a favourite with Nobel Prize-winning author Halldór Laxness. Don't miss the amazing black-sand beach.

7 Snæfellsjökull National Park

Based around an icecapped volcano, this national park extends over rough, vegetated lava fields to a coastline rich in birdlife. Hiking, skiing and exploring local villages or Vatnshellir lava cave (www.vatnshellir.is) are all possible, and you can easily circuit the park by car in a day (see pp26–7).

8 Laxárdalur
MAP C3

This pretty valley along Route 59 is the setting for Laxdæla Saga, the great tragic love story of Icelandic literature. It tells of the beautiful Guðrún Ósvífursdóttir and her four husbands: the first she divorces, but the rest perish due to witchcraft, feuding and drowning, respectively, while she becomes a nun. Only

EGIL'S SAGA

An interesting mixture of history, folklore and political allegory, Egil's Saga recounts the roller-coaster life of Egill Skallagrímsson (AD 910–990), a bully of a Viking who spent his youth fighting the Norwegians and his old age fighting everyone else, but was nonetheless a magnificent poet. A must-read, along with Njál's Saga and Laxdæla Saga.

place names from that time survive, namely the church at Hjarðarholt, and the farmsteads at Goddastaðir and Höskuldsstaðir.

9 Akranes
MAP B5

Akranes, Iceland's oldest fishing port, is a good place to experience a down-to-earth, gritty Icelandic town. Fishing is still the main industry and the harbour and processing factory survive alongside the less romantic National Cement Works. The town is famous for its sports club, Íþróttabandalag Akranes, whose football team has won the Icelandic Championship 18 times. The engaging Museum Centre (see p86) and a charming lighthouse provide good reasons to visit, though their location is a 10-km (6-mile) detour off the highway.

10 Hvalfjörður
MAP C4

Most people use the tunnel under the bay to bypass the 30-km- (19-mile-) deep Hvalfjörður and miss some classic scenery, including Glymur (see p44), Iceland's highest waterfall. Hvalfjörður means "whale fjord", after the number of whales once seen here. It was a US naval base during World War II and the red barracks are now holiday homes.

Glymur waterfall

See map on pp82–3

A DAY IN THE WEST

▶ **MORNING**

Drive north from Reykjavík around Kjalarnes, where the road is pinched between the sea and the Esja plateau. Avoid the 5-km- (3-mile-) long cross-fjord tunnel and follow Route 47 around **Hvalfjörður**. At the head of the fjord, take the 4-km (3-mile) gravel road inland to where the **Glymur** waterfall cascades down the 200-m- (656-ft-) high cliffs. Continue around Hvalfjörður to rejoin Route 1 and continue to **Borgarnes**. Spend an hour at the **Settlement Center** (see p83), delving into the lives of Iceland's Viking pioneers. Don't miss out on the spooky dioramas downstairs, retelling the tale of *Egil's Saga*. Have a quick lunch at the good-value café here.

AFTERNOON

Make **Deildartunguhver**, Europe's largest thermal spring (see p48), the first stop of the afternoon, followed by a further historical halt at **Reykholt**, taking in the Heimskringla Museum, the church and old geothermal bathing pool. From here, follow Route 518 to **Hraunfossar** and **Barnafoss** (see pp44), the latter the setting for a tragic tale of two children who drowned in the rapids here while trying to cross over a lava bridge. Both falls are small but attractive. At this point you can retrace your route or (though this is an adventurous, summer-only option) follow gravel tracks south via **Kaldidalur** to **Þingvellir** (see pp12–13) and back to Reykholt.

The Best of the Rest

1 Borg á Mýrum
MAP B4

Site of Egill Skallagrímsson's home, but nothing contemporary is left. The statue *Sonatorrek (Lament for my Dead Son)* is named after his poem.

2 Eiríksstaðir
MAP C3

Eiríksstaðir, Haukadal, 371 Búðardalur ▪ 434 1118 ▪ Open Jun–Sep 9am–6pm daily ▪ Adm ▪ www.eiriksstadir.is

The reconstructed longhouse of Viking Eiríkr Þorvaldsson, known as Eirik the Red, and his son Leifur, who explored Greenland and North America.

Sonatorrek

3 Gamla Pakkhúsið
 MAP A3 ▪ Ólafsbraut, Ólafsvík ▪ 433 6930 ▪ Open Jun–Aug 1–6pm daily ▪ Adm

This 1844 warehouse houses a café and a folk museum. Photographs and fishing memorabilia outline the town's history.

4 Berserkjahraun
MAP B3

Eyrbyggja Saga tells how a berserker was promised a local man's daughter if he cleared a path through this lava field, but was murdered once he completed the task.

5 Húsafell
MAP C4

Picturesque spread of woodland and meadows east of Reykholt, with an old church, open-air geothermal swimming pool and petrol station serving the scattered community of summer houses used by holiday-makers. Home to artist Páll Guðmundsson.

6 Surtshellir
 MAP C4

Large subterranean cave near Húsafell, named after the giant Surtur. Later used by outlaws, who hid stolen livestock here.

7 Akranes Museum Centre
MAP B5 ▪ Að Görðum, Akranes ▪ 431 5566 ▪ Open Jun–Aug: 10am–5pm daily; Sep–May: 1–5pm daily ▪ Adm ▪ www.museum.is

Folk, Mineral, Sports and Land Survey Museums all in one centre.

8 Kerlingarfjall
MAP B3

Route 56 to Stykkishólmur crosses Kerlingarfjall, a mountain said to be haunted by the ghost of a female troll, who turned to stone on her way back from a fishing expedition.

9 Stykkishólmur Church
MAP B3 ▪ Open 10am–5pm daily ▪ Adm for recitals

Shaped like an abstract ship, the church holds music recitals from June to August.

10 Glanni
MAP C4

A pretty cascade over black lava on the Norðurá salmon river near Bifröst. You can see salmon swim upstream.

Berserkjahraun lava field

Places to Eat

PRICE CATEGORIES
For a three-course meal for one with half a bottle of wine (or equivalent meal), including taxes and extra charges.
....
ⓚ under ISK5,000   ⓚⓚ ISK5,000–9,000
ⓚⓚⓚ over ISK9,000

Hótel Búðir

1 Hótel Búðir
MAP A4 ■ ⓚⓚ

Probably western Iceland's finest restaurant, serving fresh lamb and seafood dishes in a smart setting. It is cheaper than similar Reykjavík venues (see p130).

2 Hótel Hamar
MAP B4 ■ ⓚⓚ

Less formal than Hótel Búðir but with a similar menu and exceptional vistas out over the sea. The attached bar has a balcony with more beautiful views (see p130).

3 Settlement Center
MAP B4 ■ Brákarbraut 13–15, Borgarnes ■ 437 1600 ■ Open 10am–9pm daily ■ ⓚⓚ

This is a great place to enjoy an inexpensive meal – you can choose from the catch of the day, the lunch special of soup, salad and bread, or filling pasta dishes. Interesting vegetarian options too.

4 Hyrnan Snack Bar
MAP B4 ■ Brúartorg, Borgarnes ■ ⓚ

This is a popular alternative to the ever-crowded Shell petrol station canteen, nearby and a good place to grab a quick sandwich or a pizza during the day.

5 Fosshótel Reykholt
MAP C4 ■ 320 Reykholt ■ 435 1260 ■ www.fosshotel.is ■ ⓚⓚ

The top place to eat in Reykholt – although in truth there are not many alternatives. The menu offers straightforward soups and grills. Guests at the hotel also get to use the outdoor hot tubs.

6 Hótel Hellissandur
MAP A3 ■ Klettisbúð 9, Hellissandur ■ 430 8600 ■ www. hotelhellissandur.is ■ ⓚⓚ

Within sight of Snæfellsnes' slopes, this hotel restaurant provides Icelandic staples such as fish of the day and burgers, excellent coffee and cakes. The bar is open until late.

7 Hótel Glymur
MAP C3 ■ Hvalfjörður ■ 430 3100 ■ www.hotelglymur.is ■ ⓚⓚ

Smart retreat with an accomplished menu – carpaccio beef, pan-seared trout and home-made ice cream. The café serves tasty snacks.

8 Fjöruhúsið
MAP A4 ■ Hellnar, Snæfellsnes ■ 435 6844 ■ Open Jun–Nov 10am–10pm daily ■ ⓚ

Small café with good-value meals – famous for fish soup, coffee, home-made cakes and harbour views.

9 Plássið
MAP B3 ■ Frúarstíg 1, Stykkishólmur ■ 436 1600 ■ www. plassid.is ■ ⓚⓚ

Icelandic seafood, hearty burgers and tasty pizzas, plus a well-stocked bar, await at this welcoming retreat near the Stykkishólmur harbour.

10 Narfeyrarstofa
MAP B3 ■ Aðalgata 3, Stykkishólmur ■ 438 1119 ■ www. narfeyrarstofa.is ■ ⓚⓚ

Set in an old wooden building with a tiny lounge and comfortable sofas. Try the blue mussels and the home-made rhubarb cake.

See map on pp82–3 ←

🔟 The Westfjords

There is immense grandeur in the high, flat-topped mountains, brilliant blue seas and rugged coastline of the Westfjords, located in the extreme northwest of Iceland. For the region's scattered communities, life has been tough given the minimal infrastructure outside Ísafjörður, the only sizeable town. The attractions of the area are mostly strung along the west coast between the Látrabjarg bird cliffs and Ísafjörður. Though the eastern Strandir coast offers its own low-key beauty, all inland views are filled by snow-streaked plateaus. It is best to visit in summer when the roads are open: you can fly into Ísafjörður but from there you will need to drive onward.

Thermal pool, Flókalundur

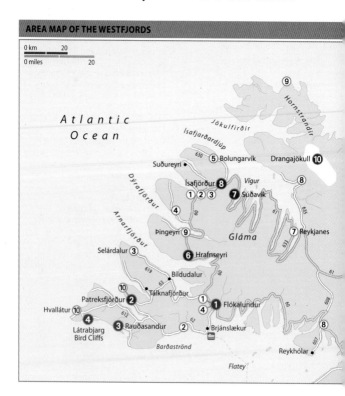

AREA MAP OF THE WESTFJORDS

Wild flowers near Patreksfjörður

1 Flókalundur
MAP B2 ■ Vatnsfjörður Nature
Reserve: www.ust.is

Flókalundur ("Flóki's Wood") is a tiny south-coast community on Route 62, named after the Viking Flóki Vilgerðarson. He endured a harsh winter here around AD 860 and, on climbing nearby Lómfell, he saw the fjord below choked with ice and gave "Ice Land" its name. The surrounding wetlands, dwarf forest and barren basalt highlands are now protected as the Vatnsfjörður Nature Reserve. You can explore it using Hótel Flókalundur (see p93) as a summertime base.

2 Patreksfjörður
MAP A2

Named after St Patrick, this comparatively sizable fishing village on Route 62 is where Iceland's trawling industry started in the early 20th century. It is famous for attacks by Basque whalers during the early 17th century. It is also the last place to stock up with provisions and fuel if you are heading to the Látrabjarg bird cliffs or the fantastic beach at Breiðavík (see p29), southwest across the fjord at the end of Route 62.

3 Rauðasandur
MAP A3

Seals are frequently seen at this cinnamon-coloured beach on the southwesternmost peninsula of the Westfjords, along the unsealed Route 614. Arctic skuas nest on the grasslands behind the spit. The ruins of Sjöundá farm lie 5 km (3 miles) east of the beach. Gunnar Gunnarsson's novel Svartfugl (Blackbird) is based on a double murder there in 1802.

4 Látrabjarg Bird Cliffs

This is among the most stirring sights in Iceland. Millions of seabirds cram into the cliffs in summer – the noise and stench are remarkable. The dramatic landscape, empty beaches and isolated buildings evoke the hardships of rural life. Local buses travel here in summer (see pp28–9).

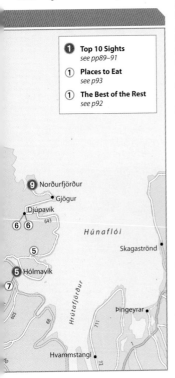

1 **Top 10 Sights**
see pp89–91

1 **Places to Eat**
see p93

1 **The Best of the Rest**
see p92

9 Norðurfjörður
• Gjögur
Djúpavík
6 6 643
5 Húnaflói
Skagaströnd
5 Hólmavík
7
Hrútafjörður
Þingeyrar •
Hvammstangi

The dramatic Látrabjarg bird cliffs

5 Hólmavík Museum of Sorcery and Witchcraft

MAP C2 ▪ Höfðagata 8, 510 Hólmavík ▪ 897 6525, 451 3525 ▪ Open Jun–mid Sep: 9am–6pm daily ▪ Adm ▪ www.galdrasyning.is

A shrimp port on the southeast coast, Hólmavík has a Museum of Sorcery and Witchcraft that draws on the district's reputation for the dark arts – during the 17th century 20 witches (only one was female) were burned at the stake. The museum has models, trinkets, an audio tour and a live demonstration of spell-casting. It runs a "Sorcerer's Cottage" 28 km (17 miles) up the coast, which shows how common people lived in the 17th century.

6 Hrafnseyri

MAP B2 ▪ 456 8260 ▪ Open Jun–Aug 10am–6pm daily ▪ Adm ▪ www.hrafnseyri.is

Hrafnseyri – a church and turf farmhouse overlooking the sea at Arnarfjörður – is of great importance as it is the birthplace of Jón Sigurðsson (1811–79), whose campaign for Iceland's independence from Denmark saw the parliament restored and a self-governing constitution enacted. His birthday, 17 June, is celebrated as National Day. The farmhouse is now a museum. Don't miss the Dynjandi waterfalls, 15 km (9 miles) to the south.

TIMBER FROM THE SEA

Iceland has always been short of home-grown timber for building boats and houses, which from Viking times has placed great demand on driftwood. Fortunately, plenty washes up around the country, particularly along the Westfjords' pebbly Strandir coast (below), whose beaches are often strewn with tree trunks that have floated all the way from Siberia.

7 Súðavík Arctic Fox Centre

MAP B2 ▪ Eyrardal, Súðavík ▪ 456 4922 ▪ Open May–Sep: 9am–6pm daily; Oct–Apr: 10am–2pm Mon–Fri ▪ Adm ▪ www.arcticfoxcenter.com

Originally the only mammal to inhabit Iceland was the Arctic fox, which probably drifted here from Greenland on ice floes. Larger than the European fox, the Arctic fox has a dark blue summer coat (which turns to white in winter) and feeds on ground-nesting birds. The Arctic Fox Centre, which is located 20 km

Dynjandi, south of Hrafnseyri

Traditional buildings, Ísafjörður

(12 miles) around the coast from Ísafjörður at Eyrardalur farm, explores the Arctic fox's biology and relationship with man.

8 Ísafjörður
MAP B2 ■ Tourist office: 450 8060; www.isafjordur.is

The region's main town, Ísafjörður is a likable place with narrow streets and old buildings. Chief among these is the Turnhús or "Tower House" (see p43), overshadowed by the steep slopes of Kirkjubólsfjall. Across the Ísafjarðardjúp straits, the uninhabited Hornstrandir peninsula offers the ultimate hiking challenge. Boats run out here and to little Vigur island (see p50) through the summer.

9 Norðurfjörður
MAP C2

At the end of Route 643 up the east Strandir coast, Norðurfjörður is small, even for the Westfjords, but the scenery is stunning and makes the drive along gravel roads worthwhile. The town is backed by the 646-m- (2,125-ft-) high Krossnesfjall hill and looks out to sea across Norðurfjörður bay. It is lonely but romantic. About 4 km (2 miles) away lies Krossneslaug, a beachside swimming pool fed by a hot spring.

10 Drangajökull
MAP B2

The area's sole permanent icecap, Drangajökull makes a splendid sight on the top of a high plateau. During the 18th century it covered local farms but has now shrunk. The best close-up view is along the dead-end Route 635 to Kaldalónsjökull, a glacier descending off larger Drangajökull. It is an hour's walk from Kaldalón (see p92).

A DAY IN THE WESTFJORDS

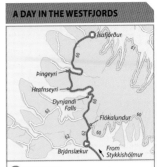

 MORNING

Arriving at **Brjánslækur** by ferry from Stykkishólmur on the Snæfellsnes peninsula (see p83), drive north up Route 62 to **Flókalundur** (see p89). Fuel up and buy something for a picnic lunch here before turning onto Route 60. This good gravel road climbs up to the Dynjandisheiði plateau and then drops abruptly to the coast at the stunning and noisy **Dynjandi** waterfall (see p45), a great place to stretch your legs and spend an hour exploring the multilevel cascades (the lighting is best here in the evening). A grassy area at the foot of the falls makes a perfect spot for a picnic.

AFTERNOON

Leaving Dynjandi waterfall, carry on around the bay to **Hrafnseyri**, birthplace of Jón Sigurðsson (see p37), and drop in at the museum celebrating the life of this great Icelandic patriot. From here it is a further 65 km (40 miles) to **Ísafjörður** via Þingeyri (the Westfjords' oldest trading town), two mountain passes and a lengthy single-lane tunnel – there are passing bays inside, but traffic is never heavy. Once at Ísafjörður, track down your accommodation and then visit the **Westfjords Maritime Museum** (see p43) inside the old Turnhús or simply stroll down to the harbour, where you can usually spot marine ducks. The nearby **Faktorshús** (see p93) is an ideal place for a late afternoon coffee and some cake.

See map on pp88–9 ←

The Best of the Rest

Djúpavík coastline

was founded as a teaching garden in 1909 by Reverend Sigtryggur Guðlaugsson.

5 Bolungarvík
MAP B1 ■ Ósvör Museum: 892 5744, 456 7005; open by appointment; www.osvor.is ■ Natural History Museum: 456 7507; www. nabo.is

This fishing port is worth a trip to see the turf buildings and wooden fishing boats at the Ósvör Museum. The Natural History Museum showcases stuffed local birds.

6 Djúpavík
MAP C2

Wild, beautiful Djúpavík, halfway along Strandir's coast, is dominated by a century-old shipwreck and a former herring processing factory that now occasionally hosts historical and art exhibitions.

7 Reykjanes
MAP B2

The hamlet of Reykjanes has a geothermal pool and sauna.

8 Kaldalón
MAP B2

Kaldalón ("Cold Lagoon") is fed by Drangajökull glacier (see p91). It inspired local musician Sigvaldi Stefánsson (1881–1946) to call himself Kaldalóns.

9 Hælavíkurbjarg
MAP B1

This vertical 258-m- (847-ft-) high cliff between Hælavík and Hornvík islets is one of the area's major bird colonies, along with Látrabjarg and Hornbjarg.

10 Hvallátur
MAP A2 ■ www.breidavik.is

Iceland's westernmost settlement comprises a farm and hotel at Breiðavík beach. It played a central role in the *Dhoon* shipwreck rescue in 1947 (see p29).

1 Pennugil
MAP B2

This narrow canyon on the Penná river is about a 30-minute walk from Flókalundur on a marked trail. There is a hot spring feeding the river which is suitable for bathing.

2 Reiðskörð
MAP A3

Route 62 runs past this tall and fragmented volcanic dyke at Barðaströnd, the bay south of the Westfjords.

3 Selárdalur
MAP A2 ■ Arnarfjörður

Self-taught artist Samúel Jónsson (1884–1969) lived in this isolated valley at the end of Route 619, and left behind a bizarre range of sculptures and buildings.

4 Skrúður
MAP A2 ■ Núpur

Set at the foot of a valley on Route 624, Iceland's oldest botanic garden

Places to Eat

PRICE CATEGORIES

For a three-course meal for one with half
a bottle of wine (or equivalent meal),
including taxes and extra charges.

Ⓚ under ISK5,000   ⒦Ⓚ ISK5,000–9,000
ⓀⓀⓀ over ISK9,000

Hótel Ísafjörður

1 Hótel Ísafjörður

MAP B2 ▪ 456 3360 ▪ ⒦Ⓚ

The hotel restaurant, Við Pollinn, has
Nordic decor and offers tasty local
fare such as catch of the day, grilled
lamb and seafood soup (see p130).

2 Faktorshús

MAP B2 ▪ Hœsti Kampstaður,
Ísafjörður ▪ 899 0742 ▪ Ⓚ

Built in 1788 and one of the country's
oldest buildings, which once housed
Ísafjörður's trading managers, it is
now a guest house with café. Its
location in a quaint part of town adds
to the charming atmosphere.

3 Hamraborg Snack Bar

MAP B2 ▪ Hafnarstræti 7,
Ísafjörður ▪ 456 3166 ▪ Ⓚ

This fast-food place serves burgers,
sandwiches, pizza and pylsur (hot
dogs) with remoulade, onions and
tomato sauce.

4 Hótel Flókalundur

MAP A2 ▪ Vatnsfirði 451,
Patreksfjörður ▪ 456 2011 ▪ Open 20
May–20 Sep ▪ www.flokalundur.is ▪
Ⓚ–⒦Ⓚ

This small restaurant has a pricey
evening menu with well-prepared
seafood and game dishes. Much
better value is the cafeteria-type
set lunch specials.

5 Hótel Laugarhóll

MAP B3 ▪ Klúka, Strandir,
Bjarnarfjörður ▪ 451 3380 ▪ www.
laugarholl.is ▪ ⒦Ⓚ

Pleasant hotel in a marvellous
setting with a thermal pool and
hiking trails within walking distance.
Its excellent restaurant has set and à
la carte menus.

6 Hótel Djúpavík

MAP C2 ▪ Djúpavík, Strandir ▪
451 4037 ▪ www.djupavik.com ▪ ⒦Ⓚ

Friendly with a fantastic location, this
hotel serves tasty, home-cooked food
in a cozy, wood-beamed dining room.

7 Café Riis

MAP C2 ▪ Hafnarbraut 39,
Hólmavík ▪ 451 3567 ▪ Open Jun–
Aug 11am–10pm daily ▪ ⒦Ⓚ

The best restaurant on the Strandir
coast, serving pan-fried puffin
breast, roast trout and lamb fillets
with panache. Also offers
sandwiches, burgers and cakes.

8 Hótel Bjarkalundur

MAP B3 ▪ Reykhólahreppi ▪
894 1295 ▪ Open 8am–10am &
11am–10pm ▪ ⒦Ⓚ

This welcoming restaurant serves
traditional Icelandic dishes made
from fresh local ingredients.

9 Simbahöllin

MAP B2 ▪ Fjarðargata 5, 470
Þingeyri ▪ 899 6659 ▪ Open mid-
May–Sep ▪ www.simbahollin.is ▪ Ⓚ

Charming café set inside an old
wooden grocery store, serving
excellent coffee, soups, stews and a
local take on Belgian waffles. The
owners also rent out horses.

10 Þorpið

MAP A2 ▪ Aðalstræti 73,
Patreksfjörður ▪ 456 1295 ▪ Ⓚ

Good grill restaurant serving the
usual fare, but the seafood is above
average, which it should be, given
the town's great seafaring heritage.

See map on pp88–9

TOP 10 North Iceland

Rich in history and wildlife and with an amazing landscape, North Iceland could easily make for a week-long trip all of its own. There is the pleasant regional capital city, Akureyri, with its fjord setting and old buildings; the glut of wildfowl and volcanic attractions around Lake Mývatn; picturesque Húsavík's laid-back charm, unusual museums and whale-watching cruises; Jökulsárgljúfur's incredible gorge system and waterfalls; not to mention a wealth of antique farms, churches and saga sites, some of them – such as Hólar – central to Icelandic history and culture. Almost all the sights in this region are located on, or easy to reach from, Route 1, making it very accessible.

Rauðhólar

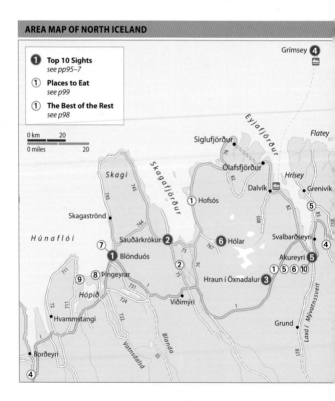

AREA MAP OF NORTH ICELAND

- **1** Top 10 Sights
  see pp95–7
- **1** Places to Eat
  see p99
- **1** The Best of the Rest
  see p98

Atmospheric old buildings, Sauðárkrókur town square

1 Blönduós
MAP D2

This port has a striking church, with steeply sloping concrete walls echoing the shape of the mountains. Other attractions include trips to see seals and birdlife in the bay and, 15 km (9 miles) west at Vatnsdalshólar, an expanse of mounds formed during an earthquake, site of Iceland's last execution in 1830.

2 Sauðárkrókur
MAP D2 ■ Drangey boat trips with Viggó Jónsson; 821 0090; May–Aug; www.drangey.net

Approached from a lush valley, Sauðárkrókur's appeal comes from the tiny knot of atmospheric old buildings that surround the town square, principally the church and Hótel Tindastóll (www.hoteltindastoll.com), which are said to be haunted. The coast here features in *Grettir's Saga*: Grettislaug, a lovely seaside thermal bathing pool, is where he recovered after swimming over from Drangey island in search of fresh embers to reignite his own fire.

3 Hraun í Öxnadalur
MAP E2

This nondescript farm in the deep Ox Valley is famous as the birthplace of poet and biologist Jónas Hallgrímsson (1807–45). His romantic verses extolling the landscape influenced the way Icelanders, most of whom then lived in poverty in rural turf buildings, began to perceive their country as glorious rather than embarrassing.

4 Grímsey
MAP E1 ■ Daily flights from Akureyri mid-Jun–mid-Aug; rest of the year: Sun, Tue & Fri only; boats from Dalvík three times a week

The only part of Iceland inside the Arctic Circle, Grímsey is 40 km (25 miles) north of the mainland, and is little more than 3 km (2 miles) long, with tiny Sandvík in the south being the only settlement. In the north, its sheer cliffs are packed with nesting seabirds in summer.

5 Akureyri

MAP E2 ■ Tourist info: www.
visitakureyri.is ■ Akureyri Museum:
Aðalstræti 58; 571 1830; www.
minjasafnid.is

Iceland's largest settlement after
Reykjavík, with a population of over
17,000, Akureyri is a relaxed town
with a pretty harbour,
shops, cafés
and restaurants.
Looming over
everything is
Akureyrarkirkja, the
huge church, with
stunning stained-
glass windows (some
brought from
England's old
Coventry Cathedral)
and modern depictions
of famous Icelanders. Don't miss the
Botanic Gardens (both native and
imported plants thrive), Davíðshús –
a museum dedicated to renowned
poet Davíð Stefánsson (1895–1964)
that exhibits his fine collection of
Icelandic art – or Akureyri Museum.

**Akurey-
rarkirkja**

6 Hólar

MAP D2 ■ Tourist office: 455
6300; open Jun–Aug 10am–10pm
daily ■ www.holar.is

More fully known as Hólar í
Hjaltadal, this was once the largest
settlement in northern Iceland

GRETTIR'S SAGA

Grettir's Saga recounts the life of Grettir
Ásmundarson, a fierce warrior who
performs great deeds in the service of
others, but is haunted by a *draugur*, or
evil ghost. Grettir ends his life as an
outlaw on Drangey island, where he is
finally killed by his enemies.

thanks to the monastery and
religious school founded in 1106 by
bishop Jón Ögmundsson, which
attracted scholars and monks from
across Europe. These institutions
survived the Reformation – which
saw the execution of Hólar's last
Catholic bishop, Jón Arason – and
today the cathedral *(see p39)* and the
college specializing in aquaculture,
rural tourism and horse science are
the sole buildings here.

7 Húsavík

MAP E2 ■ Whale-watching
tours: www.gentlegiants.is and www.
northsailing.is

Overlooking wide Skjálfandi bay,
Húsavík is Iceland's whale-watching
capital, with several daily tours
throughout summer. There is also
the superb Whale Museum and an
informative museum in the library.
The coast offers good walks along
grassy headlands and little beaches
from where you might see seals.

A whale off the coast of Húsavík

8 Lake Mývatn

Whether you have come to this country to climb cinder cones, hike your way over steaming expanses of solidified lava, bathe in open-air geothermal pools, see hot mud pools, make a day-trip into the stark Interior deserts or simply to spend some time bird-watching, you will find it all at Lake Mývatn. Although many of the sights are located around the lakeshore, you will need a vehicle in order to reach the outlying attractions, which include a flooded volcano crater known as "Hell" (see pp20–21).

Dettifoss waterfall

9 Dettifoss
MAP F2

The roads to this waterfall are gravel and open for only a few months each year. The eastern approach is easiest and traverses a stony volcanic plateau, with mountains in the distance. There is a detour well worth taking to Hafragilsfoss, a splendid waterfall just downstream, with a viewpoint inside the Jökulsárgljúfur canyon (see p44).

10 Jökulsárgljúfur
MAP F2 ■ Vatnajökull National Park: www.vatnajokulsthjodgardur.is

Set in a northern segment of the massive Vatnajökull National Park (see pp24–5), this mighty canyon is excellent for hiking, following the top of the gorge or cutting across a land rich in flowers and birdlife. Sights along the way include striking red formations at Rauðhólar, twisted hexagonal basalt columns at Hljóðaklettar, Hólmatungur's springs and Dettifoss (see p44).

A DAY IN THE LAKE MÝVATN AREA

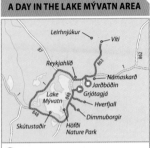

▶ MORNING

Start early, and you can just about pack all of **Lake Mývatn's** attractions (see pp20–21) into one long summer day. Begin with the subterranean hot pools at **Grjótagjá**, then move south to tackle **Hverfjall's** slippery black slopes, making a circuit of the rim for spectacular views of the whole Mývatn area. Back at ground level, **Dimmuborgir** presents an extraordinary maze of natural lava sculptures (look for rare gyrfalcons nesting on rocky towers here), with only a short drive to the lakeshore at **Höfði Nature Park**, where you will definitely encounter numerous species of waterfowl, including barrow's goldeneye, scaup and merganser. Follow the road to the south side of the lake at **Skútustaðir**, home to a large group of grassy pseudocraters.

AFTERNOON

Depending on your progress, you can grab lunch at the Dimmuborgir or Skútustaðir cafés, or circuit the lake to Reykjahlíð's **Gamli Bærinn**. Head east to the fearsome **Námaskarð** mud pits, set in a wasteland full of steam and eye-watering smells. A good side road runs north from here, via the Leirbotn Power Station, to where **Víti** volcano overlooks **Leirhnjúkur**, a huge expanse of steaming lava laid down in the 1980s – a place for careful exploration. Round off the day with a good soak on the way home at the **Jarðböðin** nature baths.

See map on pp94–5 ←

The Best of the Rest

Goðafoss waterfall

1 Hofsós

Visit the Icelandic Emigration Centre *(see p42)*, one of the country's oldest timber buildings *(Pakkhúsið)*, and have a dip in the pool *(see p59)*.

2 Glaumbær

MAP D2 ■ Glaumbær, 556 Varmahlíð ■ 453 6173 ■ Open 20 May–20 Sep 9am–6pm daily; by appointment all year round ■ Adm ■ www.glaumbaer.is

Classic turf farmhouses built between 1750 and 1879. The use of imported timber hints at the family's comparative wealth.

3 Goðafoss

This impressive waterfall is named after events that occurred when Christianity was introduced here in AD 1000 *(see p45)*.

4 Vaglaskógur

MAP E2 ■ 462 4755 ■ Camp site open May–Sep

This beautiful, extensive stretch of birch woodland along Fnjóskadalur valley is a popular camping area with a small store and walking trails.

5 Laufás

MAP E2 ■ 463 3196 ■ Open Jun–Sep 9am–5pm daily ■ Adm ■ www.laufas.is

The museum, housed in a 19th-century turf farmhouse, displays period household items. The church has a 17th-century pulpit.

6 Grenjaðarstaður

MAP E2 ■ 464 3688 ■ Open Jun–Aug 10am–6pm daily ■ Adm

Some buildings here have flowers on their turf roofs. Visit the cemetery to see headstones carved with runes.

7 Laxá í Aðaldal

Better known for its fishing potential further downstream, the Laxá's turbulent flow as it exits Lake Mývatn is a magnet for red-necked phalarope, barrow's goldeneye and harlequin duck *(see p21)*.

8 Þingeyrakirkja

MAP C2 ■ Þingeyrar, near Blönduós ■ 895 4473 ■ Open Jun–Aug 10am–5pm daily ■ Adm

Built between 1909 and 1911, this remarkable church sits alone on a vegetated sandbar *(see p39)*. A visitor centre next door runs guided tours.

9 Hvítserkur

MAP C4

This natural rock formation, which resembles a 15-m- (49-ft-) tall dinosaur drinking from the sea, lies on the east of the Vatnsnes peninsula on Route 711.

Hvítserkur rock formation

10 Tjörnes

MAP E2

This rounded peninsula with distinct banded geological strata yields bivalve and plant fossils. A signposted fossil bed is located near Ytri-Tunga farm.

Places to Eat

PRICE CATEGORIES

For a three-course meal for one with half a bottle of wine (or equivalent meal), including taxes and extra charges.

Ⓚ under ISK5,000 ⓀⓀ ISK5,000–9,000
ⓀⓀⓀ over ISK9,000

1 Hótel KEA
ⓀⓀ

The restaurant in Hótel KEA *(see p130)* offers everything from lunch buffets to à la carte dining.

2 Gamli Bærinn
MAP F2 ▪ Reykjahlíð, Mývatn ▪ 464 4170 ▪ Open May–Aug 10am–11pm daily ▪ Ⓚ

This café-bar in Hótel Reynihlíð serves beer, light meals, snacks, coffee and a legendary lamb soup.

3 Hótel Gígur
MAP F3 ▪ ⓀⓀ

This hotel restaurant *(see p130)* has beautiful views out over the pseudo-craters on Mývatn's southern shore. Serves local fish and lamb.

4 North Star Hotel Staðarflöt
MAP C3 ▪ Vegamót, Hrútafjörður ▪ 440 1336 ▪ Ⓚ

Pull up at this roadhouse located halfway on the long drive between Reykjavík and Akureyri, to stretch your legs over coffee and a burger.

5 Bautinn
MAP E2 ▪ Hafnarstræti 92, Akureyri ▪ 462 1818 ▪ ⓀⓀ

Unpretentious restaurant that serves reliably tasty grilled beef, lamb and seafood main courses.

6 Bláa Kannan
MAP E2 ▪ Hafnarstræti 96, Akureyri ▪ 461 4600 ▪ Open summer: 8:30am–11:30pm, winter: 9am–11:30 pm Mon–Fri, 10am–11.30pm Sat & Sun ▪ Ⓚ

With an unmistakable corrugated iron exterior painted dark blue, and tables spilling out onto the street, this is your best bet in town for coffee, cake and people-watching.

7 Hótel Blönduós
MAP D2 ▪ Aðalgata 6, 540 Blönduós ▪ 452 4205 ▪ ⓀⓀ

The restaurant at this hotel offers tasty, fresh home-made Icelandic food, including lamb steak, codfish, herring and rhubarb crumble.

8 Gamli Baukur
MAP E2 ▪ Harbour, Húsavík ▪ 464 2442 ▪ Open noon–8pm Sun–Wed, noon–1am Thu, noon–3am Fri & Sat ▪ Ⓚ

In wooden warehouses overlooking the harbour, this snug place serves soups and fresh fish daily, all at a reasonable cost, given the portions.

9 Salka
MAP E2 ▪ Garðarsbraut 6, Húsavík ▪ 464 2551 ▪ ⓀⓀ

Offering competition to nearby Gamli Baukur, this restaurant has a similar menu but with the bonus of outdoor tables when there is sunshine.

10 Greifinn
MAP E2 ▪ Glerágata 20, Akureyri ▪ 460 1600 ▪ Open 11:30am–9:30pm Sun–Thu, 11:30am–11pm Fri & Sat ▪ Ⓚ

A no-nonsense pizza restaurant, with an extensive menu. Takeaway options are available but it is also a lovely place to sit and eat.

Bautinn restaurant

See map on pp94–5

TOP 10 East Iceland

East Iceland covers a varied region of broad river valleys, boggy plateaus surrounding the Vatnajökull icecap, and a dramatically compressed coastline forming the East Fjords. The main centres are Egilsstaðir, on the shores of Lögurinn lake, and Höfn, a springboard for Vatnajökull National Park. Visiting smaller communities such as Vopnafjörður, Bakkagerði and Seyðisfjörður provides insight into daily life here, while rewarding side trips include Papey island and Kárahnjúkar hydro dam.

Skriðuklaustur

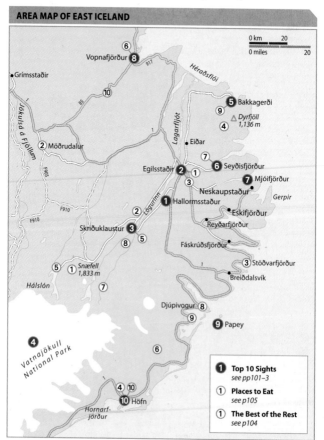

AREA MAP OF EAST ICELAND

0 km 20
0 miles 20

① **Top 10 Sights**
see pp101–3

① **Places to Eat**
see p105

① **The Best of the Rest**
see p104

1 Hallormsstaður
MAP G3

Hallormsstaður sits beside Iceland's most extensive forest, grown since the 1900s for recreational use and for timber. A web of wooded walking trails heads up the valley slopes, while a roadside Forestry Office has a small arboretum with 40 tree species including Iceland's tallest, a 22-m- (62-ft-) high larch. Near the lake is pretty Atlavík bay with scented birch surrounding the camping ground.

Hallormsstaður forest

2 Egilsstaðir
MAP G3 ▪ Summer-only buses from Akureyri and Reykjavík via Höfn; airport open year-round ▪ Museum: Jun–Sep: 11am–5pm daily; adm

Just east of Lögurinn lake, Egilsstaðir lies at the junction of Route 1 with several smaller roads to the East Fjords. A service centre offers a variety of accommodation, restaurants and well-stocked shops. Attractions include the East Iceland Museum, featuring a Viking burial site and reconstructed traditional turf houses, and the 70-km (44-mile) drive around Lögurinn taking in saga sites, extensive woodlands and one of Iceland's tallest waterfalls.

3 Skriðuklaustur
MAP G3 ▪ 471 2990 ▪ Open May–Sep: noon–5pm daily; Oct–Apr: open occasionally, call in advance ▪ www.skriduklaustur.is

This imposing villa belonging to author Gunnar Gunnarsson (1889–1975) sits on Lögurinn's western shore, close to the church at Valþjófsstaður, Hengifoss, and the road to Kárahnjúkar. Gunnarsson's series of novels about Icelandic farm life, *Af Borgslægtens Historie*, were later filmed. Besides being a Visitor Centre for Vatnajökull National Park, there is a gallery that hosts regular exhibitions. The attached Klausturkaffi offers lunch and a buffet of home-made cakes.

4 Vatnajökull National Park
MAP F4

The bulk of Europe's largest national park surrounds the Vatnajökull ice-cap, whose fringes are 100 km (62 miles) southwest of Egilsstaðir or 10 km (6 miles) northwest of Höfn. Direct access points include the Kárahnjúkur road west of Egilsstaðir, for which you will need a four-wheel drive, or hiking tracks through Lónsöræfi reserve (see p104). Skidoo trips from Höfn will bring you as far as the ice and the various glacier tongues can also be viewed from here (see pp24–5).

Vatnajökull icecap, seen from Jökulsárlón lake

Bakkagerði settlement

5 Bakkagerði
(Borgarfjörður Eystri)
MAP H2

Part of the fun of visiting Bakkagerði, the East Fjords' most endearing settlement, is the journey via the Héraðsflói estuary's grassy lagoons and steep ranges that isolate the village. On arrival you will find a tiny community backed by the jagged Dyrfjöll mountain, with sights including a little hummock near the church named Álfaborg, home to Iceland's fairy queen (according to folklore), and a sizable puffin colony overlooking the fishing harbour. Superb, lengthy hiking trails lead south to Seyðisfjörður.

6 Seyðisfjörður
MAP H3

Seyðisfjörður's charm lies in its steep fjord setting and 19th-century wooden architecture near the harbour. The church, several houses and two hotels are the pick, most painted in pastel hues and originally imported from Norway. An important naval station during World War II and a herring port before then, today Seyðisfjörður is linked to Norway by the *Norröna* ferry, which visits weekly in summer via the Faroe Islands and Denmark.

7 Mjóifjörður
MAP H3

A long, thin inlet accessed by the gravel Route 953, Mjóifjörður ("Narrow Fjord") is worth the bumpy drive to Brekka village and the remote lighthouse at Dalatangi. The road between the shoreline and steep mountains offers some close-ups of beautiful streams and cascades, plus the chance of seeing the Arctic fox, which is more at ease with humans in this remote area.

8 Vopnafjörður
MAP G2

If you are making the long coastal drive along Route 85 from Húsavík towards Egilsstaðir, set aside an hour for Vopnafjörður, a small town built on a steep prong of land. It has a museum detailing the plight of local communities following the 1875 eruption of Víti at Askja *(see p47)*. An outdoor geothermal pool at Selárdalur and Bustarfell's immaculate collection of old turf farmhouses *(see p104)* are located close by.

19th-century architecture, Seyðisfjörður

Lighthouse on Papey island

⑨ Papey
MAP H4

The ferry ride to Papey is one of the highlights of East Iceland, taking in rock ledges full of snoozing seals and seabirds flapping out of the way of boats, before reaching the small, grass-topped island, thought to have been inhabited by monks before the Vikings arrived (see p51).

⑩ Höfn
MAP G5 ■ Year-round buses to Reykjavík and summer services to Egilsstaðir; airport open year-round

Höfn started life as a warehouse during the 1860s, and developed into a small working port. It is a good base for trips to Vatnajökull National Park. The Glacier Exhibition fills you in on the area and you can book Skidoo trips and Jeep tours to the icecap. Hikers can aim for Lónsöræfi reserve. For glacier views, head for the landmark statue on the shore – avoiding the Arctic tern colony.

HÉRAÐSFLÓI'S BIRDLIFE

Héraðsflói – a broad bay with a black-sand beach and boggy meadows inland along the myriad of streamlets of the Jökulsá á Brú river – makes a superb place for observing birdlife. Look for marine ducks (including the long-tailed or old squaw and scoter), godwits, red-throated divers and even hobbys, Iceland's smallest bird of prey **(right)**.

▶ MORNING

Before starting this 70-km (44-mile) circuit of **Lögurinn lake** and the Lagarfljót valley, climb the hillock behind the Menntaskólinn school in **Egilsstaðir** for a view of the region – on a clear day you can see as far as **Snæfell** (see p104), Iceland's highest free-standing peak. Then head south, branching off the highway onto Route 931, past fields full of sheep and Icelandic horses, until a surprising amount of woodland begins to spring up around **Hallormsstaður**, where you can explore walking tracks or the Forestry Office's arboretum, or take in lakeside views at **Atlavík**. Exiting the woods past Atlavík, the main road crosses the lake to Lögurinn's west shore, where you turn left and drive some distance to **Skriðuklaustur**.

AFTERNOON

After having a snack at Skriðuklaustur's café, **Klausturkaffi**, and visiting the National Park exhibition, continue south to **Valþófsstaður** church (see p104) with its reproduction of carved Viking doors, then retrace your route back past Skriðuklaustur to where the 60-km- (37-mile-) long Route 910 ascends to moorlands around Snæfell and the **Kárahnjúkar hydro dam** (see p104). You need 3 hours for this round trip, otherwise follow an hour-long walking track uphill to Hengifoss (see p104) after parking your car. Stay on the western shore for the drive back to Egilsstaðir.

See map on pp100–1 ←

The Best of the Rest

1 Snæfell
MAP F4 ▪ www.vatnajokulsth
jodgardur.is

This isolated, snowcapped basalt core of an old volcano lies at Vatnajökull's northeast corner. It is located on a 4WD-only track. There are hiking huts around the base.

2 Hengifoss
MAP G3

This 118-m (387-ft) waterfall is Iceland's third highest, dropping in a narrow ribbon off a cliff face layered in red and black. On the way up, don't miss the twisted basalt columns at Litlifoss.

3 Steinasafn Petru
MAP H4 ▪ Sunnuhlíð, Stöðvarfjörður, East Fjords ▪ 475 8834 ▪ Open May–Sep 9am–6pm daily ▪ Adm

Extensive private geological collection, featuring coloured stones, crystals and mineral samples from all over the world. The owner does not speak English.

4 Hvítserkur
MAP H3

Spectacular orange, pink and grey rhyolite mountain 10 km (6 miles) along a hiking trail from Bakkagerði. The colours really stand out after rain. The trail is straightforward, but be prepared for changing weather.

5 Kárahnjúkar Hydro Dam
MAP F4

A controversial project that dammed the Dimmugljúfur canyon in order to provide power for a smelter. The sealed road crosses highland tundra, which is home to reindeer.

6 Lónsöræfi
MAP G4 ▪ www.vatnajokulsth
jodgardur.is

This wild, uninhabited area is rich in gorges, moorland and glacial scenery. An unmarked, 5-day trail for self-sufficient hikers runs from Stafafell to Snæfell.

7 Eyjabakkar
Boggy highland region en route to Kárahnjúkar or Snæfell, this is a breeding ground for greylag geese and whooper swans; reindeer are common too.

8 Valþjófsstaður
MAP G3 ▪ Open 10am–5pm daily

Farm and red-roofed church, with replica carved doors depicting a knight slaying a dragon. The original doors, dating from around AD 1200 are in Reykjavík's National Museum.

9 Djúpivogur Bulandsnes
MAP G4 ▪ www.djupivogur.is

Three beautiful fjords and a profusion of Icelandic wildlife make this area a nature-lover's paradise.

10 Bustarfell
MAP G2 ▪ 471 2211 ▪ Open 10 Jun– 10 Sep 10am–5pm daily ▪ Adm

Well-preserved turf-roofed farmhouses (rebuilt in 1770), occupied by the same family since 1532. Café on site.

Hengifoss

Places to Eat

Café Nielsen, Egilsstaðir

① Café Nielsen
MAP G3 ■ Tjarnarbraut 1, Egilsstaðir ■ 471 2626 ■ Open summer: 11:30am–11:30pm Mon–Fri, 1–11:30pm Sat & Sun; kitchen open to 10pm daily ■ ⓀⓀ

This restaurant-bar is housed in an old wooden building that also has an outdoor deck. The grilled fish and lamb are excellent. Try the lunch buffets, soup and salad if you need to keep the costs down.

② Fjallakaffi
MAP F3 ■ Möðrudal á Fjöllum ■ 471 1858, 894 8181 ■ Open May–Oct 7am–11pm daily ■ Ⓚ

Attached to the highest farm in Iceland (which offers accommodation), this café is reached by Route 901, south off Route 1 from Lake Mývatn.

③ Icelandair Hótel Hérað
ⓀⓀ

Local reindeer steak is the obvious dish to try at Hérað's restaurant, although they also offer lamb and seafood dishes (see p130).

④ Humarhöfnin
MAP G5 ■ Hafnarbraut 4, Höfn ■ 478 1200 ■ Open Mar–Apr & Oct: 5–9pm daily; May–Sep: noon–10pm daily ■ www.humarhofnin.is ■ Ⓚ

Look for this restaurant's distinctive orange-and-white exterior, and prepare to demolish its signature grilled langoustine tails in garlic.

⑤ Klausturkaffi
MAP G3 ■ Skriðuklaustur ■ 471 2992 ■ ⓀⓀ

This charming café serves lunches and a delicious cake buffet every day during summer.

⑥ Hótel Tangi
MAP G2 ■ Hafnarbyggð 17, Vopnafjörður ■ 473 1205 ■ ⓀⓀ

The hotel restaurant is the most popular place to eat in Vopnafjörður. Their pizzas, burgers and grilled fish are excellent.

⑦ Hótel Aldan
ⓀⓀ

Housed in a pretty wooden building in Seyðisfjörður, the restaurant in this hotel is a great place to eat an early cooked breakfast or an elegant three-course dinner. Their fish dishes are particularly outstanding (see p132).

⑧ Hótel Framtið
ⓀⓀ

Fill up on hearty fish and lamb dishes at this eatery on Djúpivogur's harbour before making the trip over to Papey island (see p130).

⑨ Álfacafé
MAP H2 ■ Bakkagerði ■ 862 9802, 472 9900 ■ Open 10am–8pm daily ■ Ⓚ

Housed inside a former fish factory near Bakkagerði's old harbour, Álfacafé has exceptionally heavy tables and crockery made out of solid stone. Only light meals are served and the sandwiches are good.

⑩ Kaffi Hornið
MAP G5 ■ Hafnarbraut 42, Höfn ■ 478 2600 ■ ⓀⓀ

Warm up inside this timber building on Höfn's main street. Fresh local seafood and Icelandic meat dishes are served on checkered tablecloths.

See map on p100

🔟 South Iceland

South Iceland has a rich band of coastline, minor icecaps, fertile river plains and explosive volcanic landscapes, all wrapped up in history and folklore. The Blue Lagoon and the "Golden Circle", which includes Þingvellir, Geysir and Gullfoss, are Iceland's most iconic sights. There is also the Hekla volcano, a wealth of saga locations, waterfalls, hiking grounds, the gem-like Westman Islands and peaceful Vík village, all in easy reach of Reykjavík. You will need more time to reach Kirkjubæjarklaustur town, the Jökulsárlón glacial lagoon and the fringes of Vatnajökull National Park.

The Blue Lagoon

1 Þingvellir National Park

This amazing rift valley, now a UNESCO World Heritage site, was the setting for Iceland's open-air parliament in Viking times. Stop at the Visitor Centre on the way along Route 36 for superlative views over the rift walls and the lava plains. Pick out key features such as the Law Rock, Þingvellir Church, Almannagjá canyon, Öxarárfoss waterfall, Þingvallavatn lake and the Skjaldbreiður volcano (see pp12–13).

Öxará river, Þingvellir National Park

AREA MAP OF SOUTH ICELAND

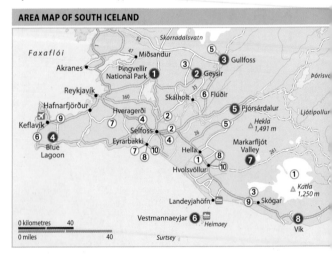

Faxaflói
Skorradalsvatn
Miðsandur
Akranes
Gullfoss
Þingvellir National Park ❶
Geysir ❷
Reykjavík
Skálholt
Flúðir ❻
Hafnarfjörður
Hveragerði
Pjórsárdalur ❺
Keflavík ✈ ❾
Selfoss
Hekla △ 1,491 m
❻ ❹
Eyrarbakki
Hella
Markarfljót Valley
Blue Lagoon
Hvolsvöllur
Katla △ 1,250 m
Landeyjahöfn
Skógar
Vestmannaeyjar ❻
Heimaey
Vík ❽
Surtsey
Þórisv
Ljótipollur

0 kilometres 40
0 miles 40

Previous pages Kirkjugólf ("The Church Floor"), Kirkjubæjarklaustur

Gullfoss, Iceland's most dramatic waterfall

2 Geysir

It is incredible to find such a raw, primal sight as Geysir's scalding waterspouts erupting by the side of the main road. Just 90 minutes from the capital, Geysir has a hotel, petrol station and tourist centre. The key geyser to watch is Strokkur, which erupts every few minutes (you would be very lucky to see the original vent, Geysir itself, blow its top, as it is very rare now). The whole site is surrounded by a collection of smaller hot pools, each with its own distinct character (see pp16–17).

3 Gullfoss

The final stop on a tour of the "Golden Circle", Gullfoss is Iceland's most dramatic waterfall and it is deafening, except in winter. Make sure you get a look at it from as many viewpoints as possible – especially from the top of the canyon, where you can appreciate the Hvítá river's journey from the barren Interior to the north (see pp18–19).

4 The Blue Lagoon

Iceland's southwest extreme, the Reykjanes peninsula, is almost entirely covered in barren lava fields, which makes finding the vivid Blue Lagoon hidden within it doubly surprising. Making creative use of waste water from a geothermal power plant, the Blue Lagoon offers an outstanding experience of outdoor soaking. Its white silt is said to have health benefits, too (see pp14–15).

5 Þjórsárdalur

MAP D5 ▪ Both access roads subject to closure ▪ Þjóðveldisbærinn: Jun–Aug 10am–6pm daily; www. thjodveldisbaer.is ▪ Þjórsárdalslaug: see www.swimminginiceland.com for latest information ▪ Adm

Þjórsárdalur is a broad, stark river valley, which was shaped by a huge eruption in 1102 of the Hekla volcano, just one ridge away to the east. The eruption buried a Viking longhouse up the valley at Stöng, which has now been excavated and is open to the public, reached via a rough, gravel track, with a full reconstruction nearby at Þjóðveldis-bærinn. There is a swimming pool in the small village of Árnes, next to the Þjórsárstofa visitor centre.

△ Hamarinn
1,573 m

△ Grímsvötn
1,719 m

Vatnajökull

Jökulsárlón

Skaftafell ●

● 10

Lómagnúpur ▲

Kirkjubæjarklaustur

Fagurhólsmýri

● 9

1 Top 10 Sights
see pp108–11

① Places to Eat
see p113

① The Best of the Rest
see p112

6 Vestmannaeyjar
MAP C6 ■ Summer: daily ferry from Landeyjahöfn; winter: daily ferry from Þorlákshöfn, flights from Reykjavík and Bakki

The Westman Islands are a string of volcanic outcrops off the south coast, which include the world's newest island, Surtsey. Heimaey, the largest and only inhabited island in the group, is famous for the 1973 Eldfell eruption, which partially buried Heimaey town and almost ended its fishing industry. Visitors can climb Eldfell's still-steaming slopes or walk around the coast in half a day. The museum Eldheimar (www.eldheimar.is) has exhibits on the Heimaey and Surtsey eruptions.Another highlight is the annual Þjóðhátíð festival held here (see p71).

NJÁL'S SAGA
This saga is a gripping account of a bloody, 50-year-long family feud revolving around the household of Njáll Þorgeirsson, in which the evil scheming of Mörð Valgarðsson causes the deaths of both Njáll and his friend Gunnar Hámundarson. The hard-boiled delivery is softened by deadpan humour and vivid insights into daily life during Viking times.

7 Markarfljót Valley
MAP D5 ■ Saga Centre: open Jun–mid-Sep 9am–6pm daily; adm; www.njala.is

To reach this pretty valley, take Route 1 to Hvolsvöllur township – where you should visit the excellent Saga Centre – and then follow the 30-km- (19-mile-) long Route 261 east. The area is central to key scenes from *Njál's Saga*, including the farm Völlur, where the tale opens, and Hlíðarendi, home to the virtuous Gunnar Hámundarson. There is a church on the hillside at Hlíðarendi today, from which you can look seawards over the valley, where landmarks like rocky Stóri-Dímon stand proud.

8 Vík
MAP D6

This peaceful seafront community of around 300 people is located below Reynisfjall's cliffs, Vík boasts a dramatic black-sand beach, great views east over the flat Mýrdalssandur black-lava desert, lively bird colonies and some towering offshore black stacks known as the Troll Rocks. Skógar and its waterfall are 30 minutes up the road (see p45) and there are more seascapes to be

View from the top of Eldfell volcano, Vestmannaeyjar

enjoyed to the west at Reynisfjall and Dyrhólaey *(see p52)*. Also close by are a number of walking tracks.

9 Kirkjubæjarklaustur
MAP E5

A tiny highway town in the middle of nowhere, Kirkjubæjarklaustur is surrounded by pseudocraters and hexagonal lava pavements known as Kirkjugólf ("The Church Floor"), with summer access to the awesome Lakagígar craters *(see p46)*. The town's name – literally Church Farm Monastery – reflects its origins in 1186 as a convent. Moving east, Skaftafell in Vatnajökull National Park *(see pp24–5)* is an hour's drive away, on the other side of the black, sandy Skeiðarársandur desert.

Icebergs at Jökulsárlón

10 Jökulsárlón
MAP G5

This is an essential stop on the long journey between Vík and Höfn. The icebergs, glacier tongue and rushing waters of Jökulsárlón – not to mention the bizarre sight of ice boulders on the beach – break the monotony of the bleak expanses of black gravel along the coastal fringes. Seals are the pick of the wildlife commonly encountered here, although there is also plenty of birdlife to look out for. Lagoon cruises lasting about half an hour are an option during the summer months *(see pp32–3)*.

A DAY IN SOUTH ICELAND

▶ **MORNING**

Begin a classic "Golden Circle" tour by heading northeast from Reykjavík up Route 36, looking out along the way for the boxy, two-storey white house of the late author and Nobel Laureate Halldór Laxness. After passing Þingvallavatn's blue expanse you arrive on the west side of the Þingvellir rift valley, where it is time to spend an hour – or the entire day – soaking up the history and landscapes at Iceland's cultural heart. Cross the rift and take Route 365 to **Laugarvatn**, where you could stop and have a swim at the National School for Sports, before pressing further along Routes 37 and 35 to spectacular water features at **Geysir** and **Gullfoss**.

AFTERNOON

Have lunch at either Hótel Geysir, where you can get a proper three-course meal, or at Gullfoss' Visitor Centre, whose café does excellent lamb soup. Then follow Route 35 southwest to **Skálholt** *(see p39)*, a bishopric and educational centre since the 11th century. Route 35 continues southwest from Skálholt past the **Kerið** crater *(see p112)* to **Selfoss**, a busy town on the Ölfusá river, where the bridge was the cause of Iceland's first strike. The highway runs straight back to Reykjavík via the hot-house town of **Hveragerði** (famous for its flowers and vegetables), or you can detour coastwards to the villages of **Stokkseyri** and **Eyrarbakki** *(see p112)*.

See map on pp108–9

The Best of the Rest

1 Mýrdalsjökull
MAP D6 ▪ www.mountain guides.is ▪ www.arcanum.is ▪ www. dogsledding.is

This impressive icecap conceals the dangerous Katla volcano. The lowest glacier tongue, Sólheimajökull, is accessible off Route 1. Here, you can ice climb or ride a snowmobile.

2 Kerið
MAP C5

This deep but small crater north of Selfoss is best viewed on a sunny day to appreciate the red and black slopes contrasting with the water.

3 Seljavallalaug
MAP D6 ▪ Seljavellir

Soak among wild scenery below the site of the 2010 Eyjafjallajökull eruption in this open-air thermal pool, tucked away at the end of a rough walking track.

4 Hveragerði
MAP C5

Hveragerði is Iceland's major greenhouse town, using geothermal heat to grow flowers and vegetables on a commercial scale. There are hiking trails and a swimming pool.

5 Leirubakki
MAP D5 ▪ Route 26 ▪ 487 8700 ▪ Summer buses between Reykjavík and Landmannalaugar ▪ www. leirubakki.is

Farm and hotel near Mount Hekla, with a volcano museum and a lava-block hot tub with views of the mountain (see p31).

6 Bridge Between Continents
MAP C5

The European and American continental plates separate visibly at Þingvellir – cross between them on this bridge, a 20-minute drive from the Blue Lagoon or Keflavík.

7 Inside the Volcano
MAP C5 ▪ Open mid-May–mid-Oct ▪ Tour duration: 5–6 hours ▪ Adm ▪ www.insidethevolcano.com

Be lowered in an open-sided cage 120 m (390 ft) into the huge magma chamber of an extinct volcano.

8 Hvolsvöllur Saga Centre
MAP C6 ▪ Hlíðarvegur 14, Hvolsvöllur ▪ 487 8781 ▪ Open summer: 9am–6pm daily; winter: 10am–5pm Sat & Sun ▪ Adm ▪ www.njala.is

Lively exhibition dedicated to the Viking era and the world of sagas.

9 Eyjafjallajökull Erupts Visitor Centre
MAP D6 ▪ Þorvaldseyri, 861 Hvolsvöllur ▪ 487 5757 ▪ Open May & Sep daily: 10am–4pm daily; Jun–Aug: 9am–6pm daily; Oct–Apr: 11am–4pm ▪ Adm ▪ www.icelanderupts.is

Exhibition on the 2010 eruption – don't miss the video of foreign reporters trying to say "Eyjafjallajökull".

10 Stokkseyri and Eyrarbakki
MAP C5 ▪ www.husid.com

Delightful villages with great seafood restaurants and the Húsið museum.

The "Inside the Volcano" tour

Places to Eat

PRICE CATEGORIES

For a three-course meal for one with half a bottle of wine (or equivalent meal), including taxes and extra charges.

Ⓚ under ISK5,000   ⒦Ⓚ ISK5,000–9,000   ⒦⒦Ⓚ over ISK9,000

1 Hótel Rangá
Ⓚ Ⓚ Ⓚ

Nordic-European cuisine is served at this splendid restaurant (see p131) with views of the finest salmon river in Iceland. Be sure to try the signature dish – salmon sous-vide.

2 Menam
MAP C5 ▪ Eyravegur 8, Selfoss ▪ 482 4099 ▪ Ⓚ

Great Thai food, cooked absolutely fresh. No MSG used.

3 Hótel Geysir
MAP C5 ▪ Haukadalur, Geysir ▪ 480 6800 ▪ Ⓚ Ⓚ

Generous breakfast and lunch buffets, an à la carte dinner menu and great views of the Geysir area make this hotel restaurant the best place to eat in the area.

4 Hótel Selfoss
MAP C5 ▪ Eyravegur 2, Selfoss ▪ 480 2500 ▪ Ⓚ Ⓚ Ⓚ

This up-market option is more comfortable than it appears, with a well-presented menu of Icelandic seafood and meat staples.

5 Gullfoss Kaffi
MAP D4 ▪ Gullfoss ▪ 486 6500 ▪ Ⓚ

With wide vistas of the surrounding landscape – though not of Gullfoss itself – this spacious, wooden-framed café is a great spot to pull up for a bowl of lamb soup.

6 Hótel Flúðir
MAP C5 ▪ Vesturbrún 1, Flúðir ▪ 486 6630 ▪ Ⓚ Ⓚ

Isolated modern building on the edge of a farming town, Hótel Flúðir has splendid views and a menu featuring locally grown greenhouse vegetables and native meats.

7 Rauða Húsið
MAP C5 ▪ Búðarstíg 4, Eyrarbakki ▪ 483 3330 ▪ Ⓚ Ⓚ

A good reason to visit the charming Eyrarbakki village, this restaurant in a historic house offers splendid lobster, lamb and fish dishes at a fraction of their cost in Reykjavík.

Lobster dish at Rauða Húsið

8 Hafið Bláa
MAP C5 ▪ Þorlákshöfn, near Óseyrar Bridge, Eyrarbakki ▪ 483 1000 ▪ Ⓚ Ⓚ

With stunning surround views, this is another excellent dining experience at the mouth of the Ölfusá river. The menu is dominated by an exceptional selection of lobster and fish dishes.

9 Kaffi Duus
MAP B5 ▪ Duusgata 10, Keflavík ▪ 421 7080 ▪ Ⓚ Ⓚ

This smart place is not far from the Keflavík International Airport, which makes it an ideal location to tuck into tasty lamb, lobster and salmon dishes before heading homewards.

10 Hlíðarendi
MAP C6 ▪ Austurvegur 3, Hvolsvöllur ▪ 487 8197 ▪ Ⓚ

This no-nonsense café inside Hvolsvöllur's main petrol station is a handy option for a pit stop after hiking in Þórsmörk with tasty burgers, pizza and good coffee.

See map on pp108–9

TOP 10 The Highland Interior

Icelandic horse, Hekla

Inland from the relatively fertile coastline, Iceland's Highland Interior is a beautiful wilderness of black gravel, lava plains and glaciated peaks, blasted by summer storms and winter frosts. Not surprisingly, the Interior is un-inhabited, but the ghosts of numerous pack-horse trails have now been graded for 4WDs only. Open for a few weeks in summer, the most accessible of these routes are the Kjölur (from Gullfoss to near Akureyri) and Fjallabak (from Hella to Kirkjubæjarklaustur). Long-distance buses follow these routes from June to September. At the moment there are also tourist flights over the ongoing eruption of Bárðabunga at Holuhraun.

AREA MAP OF THE HIGHLAND INTERIOR

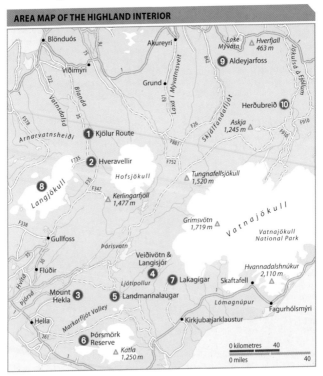

Panoramic view of the spectacular Langisjór lake

1 The Kjölur Route
MAP D4 ▪ Bus schedule: www.
bsi.is ▪ Road open mid-Jun–late Aug
▪ www.sterna.is

The Kjölur Route (Kjalvegur) is the least difficult of the Highland roads, running for 170 km (106 miles) from Gullfoss (see pp18–19) to Route 1 near Blönduós (see p95). All the major rivers have been bridged and the gravel track is safe. Sights along the way include Hveravellir's hot springs and the Langjökull icecap.

2 Hveravellir
MAP D4

Halfway along the Kjölur Route, Hveravellir is a desolate hot springs area with an outdoor hot tub, calcified mounds bubbling boiling water, a strong smell of sulphur and a basic hut with bunk beds run by the Icelandic Touring Association (www.fi.is). The 17th-century outlaw Eyvindur spent many winters here until local farmers chased him out.

3 Mount Hekla

MAP D5

East of Þjórsá river is Mount Hekla, which means "hooded", after the clouds that obscure its summit. It was once believed to be the entrance to hell, due to its eruptions followed by months of noisy "grumbling" (taken to be the sound of tormented souls). On a good day, you can see the mountain from Hella on Route 1, and you will pass close to it en route to Landmannalaugar. Many companies run Jeep circuits and trips to the mountain in summer.

4 Veiðivötn and Langisjór
MAP E5

Veiðivötn and Langisjór are part of a complex of inland waterways inside volcanic "stretch marks" southwest of Vatnajökull, reached off the F208 Fjallabak Route. There are good fishing areas amidst the stark countryside. Veiðivötn is an area of tarns and streams, while Langisjór is a narrow stretch of water. Both are accessible only along rough tracks and there is no public transport.

5 Landmannalaugar
MAP D5

Relatively accessible and just 3 or 4 hours' drive from Reykjavík, Landmannalaugar delivers a full-on Highland experience. The road takes in volcanic wastelands, exciting river crossings, mountains and hot springs. There are enough hills, lava fields and lakes to spend a day exploring. You could even stay at the bunkhouse or the camp site and spend 4 days hiking to Þórsmörk along the Laugavegur trail (see p61).

Laugavegur hiking trail, near Landmannalaugar

6 Þórsmörk Reserve
MAP D6

Iceland's most popular hiking area, accessible only by 4WD from the highway near Hvolsvöllur via the 30-km- (19-mile-) long F249 – though watch out for the potentially dangerous river crossing at the end – or by trekking in along Laugavegur or from Skógar via Fimmvörðuháls *(see p60)*. Set in an exceptionally pretty glacial valley, pick of the views at Þórsmörk are from Valahnúkur (easy and short ascent) and Utigönguhöfði (arduous and long ascent). There are plenty of self-catering cabins and camp sites, and daily buses in summer *(see p61)*.

7 Lakagígar
MAP E5 ■ Buses: Jun–Aug daily ■ Bus schedule: www.bsi.is

This 25-km- (16-mile-) long row of craters erupted with a vengeance in 1783, disrupting weather patterns all across Europe and nearly depopulating Iceland. Walking trails ranging in length between 20 minutes and 2 hours allow you to explore the line of cones and expansive lava fields, which are now partly buried under a thick matting of moss and heather. There is no accommodation on site, but mountain huts and camp sites can be found along the road. Seasonal

HIGHLAND DRIVING

Rough conditions, no settlements and nobody to help if something goes wrong all make it imperative that Highland roads are tackled only in high-clearance 4WD vehicles. Travel in convoy, check road conditions before setting out (www.vegagerdin.is) and give your route and estimated arrival time to someone reliable so rescue can be organized if needed.

buses from Skaftafell run here via Kirkjubæjarklaustur and the 60-km- (37-mile-) long F206 *(see p25)*.

8 Langjökull
MAP D4 ■ Year-round Jeep tours from Reykjavík ■ www.adventures.is ■ www.glacierjeeps.is

Iceland's second largest icecap, the "Long Glacier" west of the Kjölur Route, feeds Hvítárvatn and Sandvatn lakes, which in turn drain into the Hvítá river, on which the spectacular Gullfoss waterfalls are located *(see pp18–19)*. There is talk of damming another of Langjökull's lakes, Hagavatn, for hydropower. Apart from seeing the glacier from the Kjölur or Kaldidalur routes, tours run up here for snowmobiling trips – you only get an hour but it is an exhilarating experience, like riding a Jet Ski on snow.

Langjökull, Iceland's second largest icecap

Basalt columns at Aldeyjarfoss

⑨ Aldeyjarfoss
MAP E3 ▪ Bus schedule:
www.re.is

Although this impressive waterfall on the Skjálfandafljót river sits at the northern end of the otherwise difficult Sprengisandur Route, it is actually located on a good gravel road 30 km (19 miles) south of the Goðafoss waterfall (see p45). Most vehicles can make it with care during the summer, but check conditions first. The surrounding rock formations are what make Aldeyjarfoss so striking. A layer of outlandishly fashioned basalt columns is capped by a thick blanket of solidified lava. Buses negotiating the Sprengisandur crossing between Reykjavík and Akureyri make it a point to stop here.

⑩ Herðubreið
MAP F3

Known as the "Queen of the Mountains", Herðubreið's spiky palagonite heights rise to an impressive 1,682 m (5,518 ft) northeast of Askja, above the dismal Ódáðahraun ("Desert of Evil Deeds"). The slopes are laced with short freshwater springs and covered with the pink blooms of the Arctic river beauty flower in July. You get good views of the mountain on a clear day from the road to Kárahnjúkar (see p104), but if you fancy hiking, stop on the F88 between Mývatn and Askja (see pp20–21).

A DAY IN THE HIGHLANDS

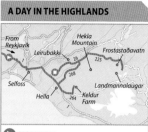

▶ **MORNING**

Start early for this day trip to **Landmannalaugar** and bring a packed lunch. The journey will take upwards of 8 hours, depending on how many times you stop along the way. Head east along Route 1 from Reykjavík via Selfoss and Hella, then turn north up Route 264 to see the Viking buildings at **Keldur** farm. With **Hekla** looming behind, take a moment to appreciate Keldur's location – so close to an active volcano. Retrace the route towards Hella, then turn north along Route 268 for a half-hour run through lava fields to Hekla and the intersection with Route 26. You could turn left here to **Leirubakki** farm (see p112), but for Landmannalaugar turn right, driving across the yellow pumice plain between Hekla and the Þjórsá river, before reaching the junction with F225, which heads east to Landmannalaugar. Pull up and enjoy your picnic lunch.

AFTERNOON

The F225 road traverses the black-sand wasteland of Hekla's northern foothills, with several river crossings before it reaches an intersection after 47 km (29 miles). Turn right (south) at this junction, which leads down to **Frostastaðavatn**'s lakeshore and then right again onto the 5-km- (3-mile-) long F224, which crosses a double fjord before reaching Landmannalaugar. Soak in the spring and then prepare to head back. Once you are on Route 26, simply follow it south to the **Vegamót** roadhouse between the towns of Hella and Selfoss.

See map on p114 ←

Streetsmart

**Mount Esja dominating the
Reykjavík skyline**

Getting To and Around Iceland

By Air

Most flights from Europe, the USA and Canada land at **Keflavík International Airport**, 50 km (31 miles) from Reykjavík. The national carrier is **Icelandair**, but you may get better deals with budget operators like **WOW Air**. It takes about 3 hours to reach Iceland from Europe and 5–6 hours from the USA. The cheapest way into town from Keflavík is the **Flybus**, which delivers arrivals to the **BSÍ** long-distance bus station and major hotels in Reykjavík in about 45 mins. Taxis are expensive, but you can arrange to collect rental cars at the airport.

Some flights from Greenland and the Faroe Islands use **Reykjavík International Airport**, just west of the city centre (there are plans to relocate it after 2016).

Reykjavík International Airport also offers direct domestic flights with **Air Iceland** and **Eagle Air** to Akureyri, Egilsstaðir, Húsavík, the Westman Islands, Ísafjörður, Höfn, Sáuðárkrókur, Gjögur and Bíldudalur. From Akureyri, there are connections to Grímsey, Vopnafjörður and Thorshöfn. Both airlines offer day trips and adventure tours. Regional airports generally stay open in winter, when roads might be closed.

By Sea

From April until the end of October, the **Smyril Line** runs a weekly passenger and vehicle ferry between Denmark and Seyðisfjörður in eastern Iceland. It costs more than flying, and the 3-day crossing can be rough, but you get the chance to visit the Faroe Islands en route and it's the only way to bring your own vehicle into Iceland. International cruise boats also visit Iceland during the summer, docking at Reykjavík, Akureyri, Ísafjörður and Seyðisfjörður.

Ferries run to a number of offshore islands. Daily services to the **Westman Islands** go from Landeyjahöfn in the south (about 30 mins). Ferries also run to **Grímsey** and **Hrísey** in the north, and **Stykkishólmur–Flatey–Brjánslækur** in the west.

By Bus

Strætó serves Reykjavík and its suburbs as far as Selfoss, Akranes and Hafnarfjörður (7am–midnight Mon–Sat, noon–midnight Sun). The flat fare is ISK350 (you pay the exact amount when boarding), but day and multi-day discount cards are available at the Hlemmur bus station.

From the BSÍ station, **Reykjavík Excursions** run day tours in the south and west of Iceland. During the summer they run the **Iceland On Your Own** bus services in cooperation with **SBA-Norðurleið**, serving most of Iceland. Similar operators include **Sterna Travel** and **TREX** in Reykjavík. Other parts of the country are covered by local operators. While most destinations are served daily in summer, all Interior services, even those along the Ringroad between Höfn and Egilsstaðir, stop or are reduced at other times.

Passes that restrict you to a specific route and schedule are the more economical, than paying for separate journeys. Book bus seats at least a day in advance.

By Car

You can bring your car to Iceland on the Smyril Line ferry from Denmark. There are plenty of car-rental agencies, such as **Iceland Car Rental**, though rates are high. The minimum age for renting a car is 20 (25 for Jeeps). Rental cars might not be insured for some routes. Seatbelts are compulsory and headlights must always be on. Driving is on the right-hand side. Speed limits are 90 kmph (56 mph) on asphalt roads, 80 kmph (50 mph) on gravel roads and 30 kmph (19 mph) in residential areas. Drink-driving and driving off marked roads or tracks are illegal.

Reykjavík's main roads can become gridlocked during rush hour (7:45–9am and 4–6:30pm). Route 1, or the Ringroad, runs a circuit 1,300 km (808 miles) around the country, but it is fairly narrow. Many country roads are unsealed gravel and not suited to fast driving. Roads marked on a map with an F require four-wheel-drive at all times. Bad weather can make any road dangerous for conventional vehicles. Many four-wheel-drive routes cross dangerous rivers, snowfields and sands, and are suitable for experienced drivers only. Some car-rental agencies offer GPS rental.

By Taxi

Taxis in Iceland are metered and have uniform fares. There is no tipping. Look for ranks outside major hotels or call for one. Taxis to Keflavík International Airport have fixed rates: ISK13,000 for 1–4 passengers or ISK16,000 for 5–8 passengers.

By Bicycle

Cycling is an inexpensive way of seeing the country in summer, though come prepared for unsealed gravel roads and unkind weather. You need to be fit, experienced in repairing your bike, and to carry spares. You also need a tent and cooking gear and supplies, as there can be considerable distances between towns. There are several bike-hire shops in Reykjavík and Akureyri, but little assistance elsewhere. It is only permitted to cycle on roads or marked tracks.

By Foot

Iceland has many hiking trails. Accommodation is either camping or using hiking-organization huts. Both need to be pre-booked. Come equipped for bad weather and rough terrain (including river crossings). Carry all necessary gear, such as food, water and maps or a GPS. Some routes may also require crampons and an ice axe. Iceland's two hiking organizations, **Útivist** and **Ferðafélag Íslands**, can offer advice.

By Horse

Iceland's unique, stocky horses arrived with the Vikings. In addition to walk, trot, gallop and canter, they have a "fifth gear", the tölt. Stables like **Íshestar** and **Eldhestar** offer everything from hour-long to multi-week expeditions.

DIRECTORY

AIRPORTS

Domestic Airports
🖳 isavia.is

Keflavík International Airport
🖳 kefairport.is

Reykjavík International Airport
🖳 isavia.is

AIRLINES

Air Iceland
🖳 airiceland.is

Eagle Air
🖳 eagleair.is

Icelandair
🖳 icelandair.com

WOW Air
🖳 wowair.co.uk

FERRIES

Grímsey and Hrísey
📞 458 8000
🖳 landflutningar.is/saefari

Smyril Line
📞 298 354 900
🖳 smyrilline.com

Stykkishólmur–Flatey–Brjánslækur
📞 433 2254
🖳 seatours.is

Westman Islands
📞 481 2800
🖳 eimskip.is/en

BUSES

BSÍ
📞 562 1011
🖳 bsi.is

Flybus
📞 580 5400
🖳 re.is/flybus

Reykjavik Excursions
📞 580 5400
🖳 re.is

SBA-Norðurleið
📞 550 0700
🖳 sba.is

Sterna Travel
📞 551 1166
🖳 sterna.is

Strætó
📞 540 2700
🖳 straeto.is

TREX
📞 587 6000
🖳 trex.is

CAR TRAVEL

Iceland Car Rental
📞 415 2500
🖳 icelandcarrental.is

Road Conditions
🖳 vegagerdin.is/english

TAXIS

Taxi Reykjavík
📞 561 0000
🖳 taxireykjavik.is

HIKING

Ferðafélag Íslands
🖳 fi.is/en/home

Útivist
🖳 utivist.is/english

HORSE RIDING

Eldhestar
🖳 eldhestar.is

Íshestar
🖳 ishestar.is

Practical Information

Passports and Visas

Visitors from the UK, Ireland, Canada, the EU, the USA, Australia, New Zealand and countries that are signed up to the Schengen Agreement do not need a visa for Iceland for a visit under 90 days. To enter the country, your passport must be valid for 3 months beyond the date of your intended stay.

Travel Insurance

Iceland is a relatively safe country, but it is advisable to take out travel and health insurance. Check any policy exclusions, especially if planning on hiking or adventure travel. Also check any home polices you have as you may already be covered through your bank.

Customs Regulations and Immigration

Passengers over 18 may import 200 cigarettes or 250 g (8.8 oz) of tobacco products. Those over 20 may also bring a litre of spirits, a litre of wine and 6 litres of beer. Visitors can import 3 kg (7 lb) of food duty-free, but no meat unless canned or boiled. Riding clothing and angling gear must be disinfected and certified by a vet before entry. Used riding gear cannot be brought.

Vehicles, with up to 200 litres (44 gal) of fuel in built-in fuel tanks, can be brought in tax-free on the Smyril Line ferry to Seyðisfjörður, providing that you live overseas, stay less than a year in Iceland, use the vehicle for personal travel only and take it with you on leaving. European drivers who bring their own vehicles do not need a Green Card or proof of third-party insurance; otherwise, international automobile insurance may be required. Check with **Icelandic customs**.

Tourist Information

Good sources of general tourist information include the official websites of the **Iceland Tourist Board**, **Promote Iceland**, **Randburg Travellers' Guide**, **Vatnajökull National Park**, **Visit Reykjavík**, **Visit Akureyri** and **Iceland Today**. For hikers and anglers, the website of **Nordic Adventure Travel** will be useful.

Health and Safety

No vaccinations are required for Iceland. You are advised to bring all medications you might need with you. All EU citizens holding an EHIC card are eligible for the same level of state healthcare as they would receive at home, but US and other citizens have to pay. Ambulances incur a nonrefundable cost. Pharmacies *(apótek)* are in almost every town and often stay open until late. Prescription prices vary. Tap water is safe to drink everywhere in Iceland. Bring warm, wind- and waterproof clothes as the weather can be unpredictable. You'll also need sunglasses, sunscreen and a hat, especially if you are planning to hike or spend time outdoors. Hikers need tough boots for lava, snow and rain.

Be aware of natural hazards: you'll find very few warning signs or safety barriers even at heavily touristed sights such as waterfalls, geysers or boiling mud pits. Unbridged river crossings are dangerous, whether on foot or in a vehicle. Hiking trails are often poorly marked; hikers should be competent at navigation in poor conditions. Avalanches have claimed many lives in Iceland over the years; you should always check warnings before hiking, especially in the West and East Fjords. If swimming, be aware that the coastline and beaches are typically not guarded.

Personal Security

Iceland is a safe country, with a low crime rate, but the usual advice applies. Always lock your car, don't leave valuables on display and don't flash your cash. Keep an extra eye on your belongings when you are in crowds, on public transport or queuing at busy tourist attractions. Minor assaults, petty burglary and drug-related crimes do occur, primarily in Reykjavik. Women in particular should take special care in busy bars and clubs late at night and around the Hlemmur bus station. Otherwise, sexual harassment is not a common problem.

Penalties for possession, use and trafficking of drugs are severe, with large fines and custodial sentences. Iceland's police officers (lögreglan) carry pepper spray and extendable batons but, with the exception of airport police, no firearms.

Currency and Banking

Iceland's currency is the króna (ISK) or krónur in the plural. You can bring up to the equivalent of €10,000 into the country. Foreign currency is accepted at Keflavík International Airport and in a few shops in Reykjavík. Banks are found in all major towns, many with 24-hour ATMs outside issuing krónur. You'll also find ATMs in larger stores, malls and at petrol stations. MasterCard and Visa are widely accepted by ATMs and businesses across the country but many places won't handle American Express, or accept cards to pay for purchases totalling less than ISK500. Check with your local bank before travelling to see if you can use your card abroad, and to find out the surcharges that will be levied to your account.

Opening Hours

Office hours are 9am–5pm Monday–Friday, changing to 8am–4pm during the months of June, July and August. Shops are open 10am–6pm Monday–Friday, and Saturday from 10am until between 1pm and 4pm. Some supermarkets are open daily until 11pm. Banks are open 9:15am–4pm Monday–Friday. Outside Reykjavík, the hours may be shorter. Museums have their own opening hours, and outside the capital they might be closed in winter.

Businesses, banks and most shops are closed on the following holidays: New Year's Day, Maundy Thursday, Good Friday, Easter Sunday, Easter Monday, First Day of Summer (usually third Thursday in April), Labour Day (1 May), Ascension Day, Whit Sunday, Whit Monday, National Day (17 June), Bank Holiday (first Monday in August), Christmas Eve (from noon), Christmas Day, 26 December and New Year's Eve (from noon).

Time Zone

Iceland follows Greenwich Mean Time and is 5 hours ahead of US Eastern Standard Time. It does not observe Daylight Saving Time.

Electrical Appliances

Iceland has standard European electrical voltage and frequency (240 V, 50 Hz) so North American electrical devices will need converters. Plugs are European-style two-pin. UK and North American electrical items will need a special adapter.

DIRECTORY

VISAS AND CUSTOMS

Icelandic Customs
w customs.is

Visas
w utl.is

EMBASSIES

Canada
MAP K2 ■ Túngata 14, Reykjavík
w canada.is

UK
MAP L3 ■ Laufásvegur 31, Reykjavík
w britishembassy.is

USA
MAP L3 ■ Laufásvegur 21, Reykjavík
w iceland.usembassy.gov

TOURIST INFORMATION

Iceland Today
w icelandtoday.is

Iceland Tourist Board
w visiticeland.com

Nordic Adventure Travel
w nat.is

Promote Iceland
w iceland.is

Randburg Travellers' Guide
w randburg.is

Vatnajökull National Park
w vatnajokulsthjodgardur.is/english

Visit Akureyri
w visitakureyri.is/en

Visit Reykjavík
w visitreykjavik.is

EMERGENCY SERVICES

Police, Fire and Ambulance
c 112

Akureyri Hospital
Eyrarlandsvegur
c 463 0100

Landspítali University Hospital
MAP M4 ■ Norðurmýri, 101 Reykjavík
c 543 1000

Driving Licences

All European and US driving licences are valid in Iceland. UK visitors need to bring both parts of their licence. Visitors from other countries should check what they need with their local motoring organizations.

Fuel

Fuel is priced by the litre. Self-service pumps are cheaper than attended ones. Atlantsolía (AO) and ÓB are the cheapest brands. Fill up when you can in rural areas, as smaller towns might not have pumps and the gaps between filling stations can be large. Most filling stations are open until 11:30pm. Those in Reykjavík and large towns often have automatic payment available after closing time, which accepts notes and Visa credit cards. Some pumps in the countryside are completely automated.

Communications

Iceland's country code is 354; phone numbers within Iceland are seven digits long, with no area codes. All domestic calls are charged at a local rate, cheapest 7pm–8am Monday–Friday. Overseas calls are cheaper 7pm–8am every day for Europe and 11pm–8am every day for elsewhere. In the phonebook, people are listed in order of first name, not surname. The mobile phone network is reliable along the coast. It is a GSM system, compatible with European networks but not US

ones. Buy a prepaid local SIM card if yours doesn't work here. Central Iceland has Nordic Mobile Telephone (NMT) coverage, but you should only need this if you're travelling independently in the Interior. Contact vehicle-rental companies or hiking organizations about renting an NMT set.

Iceland has one of the world's highest per capita internet usage rates. Free Wi-Fi is available in many cafés and in some accommodation. Tourist offices and libraries usually have computers available for public use.

Post offices are found in most major towns and are open 9am–4:30pm Monday–Friday, sometimes closing later in larger towns. Stamps are also sold in hotels, bookshops and supermarkets.

There are nine free TV channels in Iceland. Much of the content is in English and subtitled. Many hotels have satellite TV and screen major sporting events such as international and Premiership football.

Morgunblaðið, *Fréttablaðið* and *DV* are the main Icelandic newspapers. Both *Morgunblaðið* and *Fréttablaðið* have English summaries of the news on their websites. *Iceland Review* is a monthly English-speaking lifestyle magazine with a heavy tourist slant. Its website also offers a roundup of news stories. Free English-language newspaper *Grapevine* offers a lively view of the day's major issues, and is also a good what's-on guide for Reykjavík.

English-language newspapers and magazines are available in hotels and bookshops, or for free in libraries.

Weather

Iceland's summer sun barely dips below the horizon at midnight. In winter you are lucky to get 4 hours of daylight, making November to February perfect for watching the aurora borealis. The climate is milder than you might expect. In the south of the country, winters average a bearable 0°C (32°F), while summer temperatures can reach 23°C (74°F), though rains can be frequent from spring to autumn. The north is generally much colder, with heavy snowfalls in winter and temperatures dropping below -15°C (5°F), though the northeast is famously sunny in summer. The centre of the country is dominated by Vatnajökull, Europe's largest icecap, and the Highland Interior is uninhabited and usually snowbound for much of the year. Roads only open for a few weeks from mid-July until September.

Maps

Forlagið and Ferðakort publish road atlases and specialist maps that cover the country in great detail and are useful for independent touring and hiking. You can buy a good range at bookshops in Reykjavík and Akureyri, plus a restricted selection at some tourist offices, supermarkets and roadhouses.

Hiking organizations and the Icelandic National Parks office publish local maps, which are usually only available on site.

Disabled Travellers

Iceland is fairly aware of the needs of disabled travellers, with urban hotels, restaurants, businesses and transport links either accessible or able to provide the relevant services if notified in advance. Reykjavík's Association for Disabled People, **Sjálfsbjörg** does not directly cater to tourists, but may provide advice.

Swimming

Make sure you bring your swimming gear to Iceland. Every town has a public pool *(sundlaug)*, geothermally heated to a constant temperature of 28°C (83°F) and often with attached hot tubs and saunas. They are inexpensive, and many Icelanders spend hours at them every day. There is a strict pool etiquette to be followed: make sure you take your shoes off before entering the changing rooms, leave your towel on the racks between the changing rooms and the pool so you can dry yourself before returning to dress, and shower without your costume before entering the pool area.

Out in the wilds, there are also many natural geothermal springs in places such as Landmannalaugar and Mývatn, not to mention the artificial Blue Lagoon, which offer a fantastically atmospheric experience, especially during the winter months.

Smoking

Smoking is prohibited in bars, restaurants, clubs and cafés. There are no designated smoking areas inside and smoking outside is also restricted to certain areas. It is forbidden to smoke on public transport.

Shopping

Imported goods will be more expensive than they would be at home, but a number of local products make good-value souvenirs. Icelandic woollen jumpers are available from shops but, as many are home-made, sizes and proportions can be random and you'll have to try on several until you find a good fit.

Smoked salmon, trout and Arctic char are excellent and cheapest if bought at supermarkets or directly from smokehouses. You'll need to check that you're allowed to import them into your home country.

Outdoor clothing by 66°N and Cintamani is stylishly designed and of high quality, though not cheap. Silver and lava jewellery is also popular. Note that anything made from sealskin cannot be imported into the US, though there are no such restrictions in the UK and Europe.

While there are no regular sale periods, shops tend to reduce prices in midsummer and in January. There are duty-free shops at Keflavík International Airport, where you can buy alcohol at significantly reduced rates.

All prices include VAT, which on most goods is 25.5%. Tourists get a 15% tax refund on single items costing ISK4,000 or more. To get the refund, you need to get the shop to fill out a refund form when you are buying, then take the form and receipt to a refund booth at Keflavík airport, Seyðisfjörður ferries, the Reykjavík tourist office or any Reykjavík shopping mall.

DIRECTORY

COMMUNICATIONS

Fréttablaðið
ⓦ visir.is/news

Grapevine
ⓦ grapevine.is

Iceland Review
ⓦ icelandreview.com

Morgunblaðið
ⓦ mbl.is/frettir/english

Reykjavík Central Post Office
MAP L2 ▪ Íslandspóstur, Pósthússtræti 5, 101
ⓒ 580 1200
ⓦ postur.is

WEATHER

Weather Forecast (in English)
ⓒ 902 0600

Weather Updates
ⓦ en.vedur.is

DISABLED TRAVELLERS

Sjálfsbjörg Association for Disabled People
ⓒ 550 0360
ⓦ sjalfsbjorg.is

SHOPPING

Tax Refund Information
ⓦ customs.is

Trips and Tours

The **Golden Circle** tour run by Reykjavík Excursions is a classic combination of history and landscape, all within a stone's throw of Reykjavík. It takes in the Geysir hot springs, Gullfoss waterfalls and Þingvellir National Park. Reykjavík Excursions also run tours to **Lakagígar**, one of the world's largest lava fields and site of the terrible 1783 eruption.

Askja, a hellish landscape of steaming volcanic craters in the northeast Interior, is where astronauts once trained for their moon landings and makes for an interesting day trip from Lake Mývatn.

For mountain trekking, try an introductory morning of ice climbing or a hardcore ascent of Hvannadalshnúkur (Iceland's highest peak) with specialist tour company **Icelandic Mountain Guides**.

Take a half-day **whale-watching** cruise from Húsavík in the northeast, or for **puffin watching**, catch a boat out to Lundey or Akurey near Reykjavík for a sight of these entertaining and charismatic seabirds.

Language

Icelandic is a difficult, complex language, with grammar similar in some ways to German or Latin, and few foreigners even attempt to learn it. Fortunately, English is taught in Iceland from an early age and most people speak it well, although Icelanders will be ecstatic if you can manage to squeeze out even a single sentence in their mother tongue.

Dining

There is some excellent local food, worth perhaps splashing out for once in a smart restaurant. Seafood is top of the list, with superb Atlantic salmon, cod, trout and char, not to mention lobster. Icelandic lamb is also very good. At certain times of the year you can find oddities such as smoked puffin, traditionally harvested in southern Iceland, though populations are plummeting and there has been an embargo on catching these birds. Other traditional foods include *harðfiskur* (wind-dried cod), a popular snack sometimes eaten with butter; *hangikjöt* (smoked lamb); *rjúpa* (ptarmigan), a grouse-like game bird; *súrmatur* (meats pickled in whey); and *hákarl* (fermented shark), an eye-wateringly pungent speciality.

There are smart but expensive restaurants in Reykjavík, Akureyri and other large towns. You can keep costs down by sticking to the specials board or a fixed menu if available. There are less pricey Thai, Indian, Italian and Chinese places, where you can eat without bankrupting yourself, but the food is not particularly memorable. Many places offer kids portions. It is not customary to leave a tip however a service charge will be included in the final bill.

There are cafés all over the country – Reykjavík even has its own chain, Kaffitár. They often allow at least one free refill. Aside from cafés, the cheapest places to eat out are roadhouse restaurants, which are sometimes the only places serving cooked food in an area. Their menus are filling rather than exciting – pizza, burgers, chips and *pylsur* (hot dogs) – but there's usually an inexpensive set menu featuring soup and bread, often with a free refill. Museums and cultural centres often have bargain-priced eateries serving lunch and coffee – no entry fee required to dine here.

In terms of self-catering, Bónus, Krónan, Samkaup and Kjarval are the most widespread supermarkets, with Bónus charging the lowest prices. Most villages will have somewhere to stock up, but the range might be limited and opening hours are often short in the countryside. In winter, supermarkets sometimes provide free coffee for shoppers. In summer, fresh vegetables are easily available, especially in hothouse towns, where they are grown using geothermal methods. Many villages have bakeries, but rarely butchers or fishmongers.

Drinking

Alcohol is sold through state-controlled shops (Vínbúðin) and is highly taxed; you'll save money by bringing in your full duty-free allowance.

Vínbúðin have very restricted, totally unpredictable opening hours, and outside Reykjavík tend to be tucked away in obscure corners. The local spirit of choice is *brennivín* – basically, vodka flavoured with caraway and angelica. Iceland imports all of its wine, with the exception of one brand, Kvöldsól, which is made in Húsavík from blueberries, crowberries and rhubarb. The cheapest beer brands are the locally brewed Viking Gold and Thule. Because of the cost of alcohol, it is considered normal not to buy rounds, and even to sip on one drink for the entire evening, though many bars have happy hours. Locals often drink at home before going out for the night.

Accommodation

Iceland's rapidly increasing popularity has put a pressure on summer accommodation. It is wise to book beds in advance – even for hostels . Online booking is the norm everywhere.

Though you can camp for free anywhere outside metropolitan areas or national parks, most people opt to use the well-equipped and inexpensive camp sites found in even the smallest village. Most have toilets and showers. If there are no showers, head to the nearest public swimming pool. Make sure you have a weatherproof tent, a groundsheet, guy ropes and a variety of pegs, as rough ground and gale-force winds are a fact of life. In popular hiking areas you will also find mountain huts run by the hiking organizations. These are usually chalet-style buildings, with dormitories, kitchens, toilets, showers and bunks or mattresses. Beds must be booked in advance and bring a sleeping bag.

There are 32 official **hostels**, ranging from a turf-roofed hut to multi-storey affairs with TVs, kitchens, cafés and tour desks. Hostel members get a discount on the room rate. Dormitories are the norm, but some have private rooms. Bring a sleeping bag or hire bedsheets if available.

Part-way between hostels and hotels, urban guesthouses and rural **farmstays** offer a broad range of self-catering facilities, sometimes in a main building, sometimes in separate chalets. Doubles or family rooms with made-up beds are usual, though some places offer a cheaper-rate option of sleeping bag accommodation, where you supply your own bedding. Meals can usually be arranged in advance for an extra charge.

Every town in Iceland has a hotel of some sort. Many formal hotels open year-round and tend to be stuffy affairs, run by the airlines or a local company. Privately run businesses tend to have far more character. They are usually warm, well-equipped places with restaurants, bars and sometimes conference facilities, but peak summer rates are very expensive for what you get. International airlines can offer attractive flight-and-accommodation packages and you'll find that prices drop considerably outside the main summer tourist season. An alternative is to use one of the 12 summer-only **Hotel Eddas** scattered around the country, which serve as schools for the rest of the year. Rates are lower than ordinary hotels and although rooms are functional, facilities are not too bad, often with restaurants or cafés, swimming pools and even local tours available.

Places to Stay

PRICE CATEGORIES
For a standard double room per night (with breakfast if included), including taxes and extra charges.

Ⓚ under ISK20,000
ⓀⓀ ISK20,000–40,000
ⓀⓀⓀ over ISK40,000

Hotels in Reykjavík City Centre

Hótel Leifur Eiríksson
MAP M3 ▪ Skólavörðustíg 45 ▪ 562 0800 ▪ www. hotelleifur.is ▪ Ⓚ
Situated across the road from the magnificent Hallgrímskirkja, this small boutique hotel has great views of the church and nearby streets from its upper rooms. The rooms do not have a huge amount of space, but it is unquestionably good value for money.

Fosshotel Lind
MAP N3 ▪ Rauðarárstígur 18 ▪ 562 3350 ▪ www. fosshotel.is ▪ ⓀⓀ
A reliable, comfortable hotel with good facilities and helpful staff. There is nothing lacking in the services offered, but the rooms are on the small and simple side. However, it is good for a brief stay.

Hótel Frón
MAP M3 ▪ Laugarvegur 22A ▪ 511 4666 ▪ www. hotelfron.is ▪ ⓀⓀⓀ
A variety of good accommodation is on offer at this welcoming hotel, from en suite single and double rooms to apartments with kitchenettes and all the usual services, plus Wi-Fi. The decor has an efficient, modern look and the emphasis in the restaurant is on Nordic cuisine. There is a nice terrace café, too.

Hótel Klöpp
MAP M2 ▪ Klapparstígur 26 ▪ 595 8520 ▪ www. centerhotels.com ▪ ⓀⓀ
This is a streamlined place with comfortable rooms and open-plan bathrooms. Friendly, efficient and located just off bustling Laugarvegur, it is a sound option for a short stay. Rooms on the upper floors are quieter and some have sea views.

Hótel Óðinsvé
MAP L3 ▪ Þórsgata 1 ▪ 511 6200 ▪ www. hotelodinsve.is ▪ ⓀⓀ
Excellent value family-owned hotel that manages to balance the homey 1930s building with modern minimalist chic. Its location off the main streets means less likelihood of being disturbed by rowdy weekend merrymakers. The bistro-style SNAPS restaurant specializes in grills.

Hótel Borg
MAP L2 ▪ Pósthússtræti 11 ▪ 551 1440 ▪ www. hotelborg.is ▪ ⓀⓀⓀ
Wonderful Art Deco building where old time elegance and modern style is reflected in the immaculate rooms, which are a showcase in sophistication, complete with genuine period furnishings and luxurious facilities such as heated bathroom marble floors.

Hótel Holt
MAP L3 ▪ Bergstaðastræti 37 ▪ 552 5700 ▪ www. hotelholt.is ▪ ⓀⓀⓀ
Holt's unappealing façade is deceptive; once through the doors you are in one of the most plush old-style hotels in town. It has the country's largest privately owned collection of 19th-century Icelandic artworks and an outstanding restaurant.

Hótel Plaza
MAP K2 ▪ Aðalstræti 4 ▪ 590 1400 ▪ www.plaza.is ▪ ⓀⓀⓀ
Light, airy, modern building with rooms to match – timber flooring and white walls and furnishings. The suites have views of the older part of the city and there is an excellent choice of good restaurants nearby.

Hótel Reykjavík Centrum
MAP K2 ▪ Aðalstræti 16 ▪ 514 6000 ▪ www. hotelcentrum.is ▪ ⓀⓀⓀ
A modern hotel in an old building on an ancient site: the timber and red-corrugated-iron exterior sits above the remains of a 7th-century Viking settlement. The rooms have been tastefully modernized and there is a renowned restaurant.

Reykjavík 101
MAP L2 ▪ Hverfisgata 10 ▪ 580 0101 ▪ www.101hotel.is ▪ ⓀⓀⓀ
Close to the capital's main shopping street, this

smart hotel is stark on the outside. Inside, the modern, bright rooms have a contemporary minimalist look, complete with wooden flooring, large beds and marble bathrooms. Amenities include a gym and spa.

Hotels Around Reykjavík

Hótel Cabin
MAP N3 ■ Borgartún 32, 105 Reykjavík ■ 511 6030 ■ www.hotelcabin.is ■ Ⓚ
Tidy budget hotel with basic but clean furnishings and relatively compact, recently renovated rooms. Upper floors have ocean views, while some rooms are designed with inward-facing windows for relief during the bright summer nights. Great-value lunch buffet at the restaurant.

Hótel Laxnes
MAP Q5 ■ Háholt 7, 270 Mosfellsbær ■ 566 8822 ■ www.hotellaxnes.is ■ Ⓚ
A hotel in a semi-rural location, about a 20-minute bus ride from Reykjavík, near the former home of novelist Halldór Laxness. The double rooms and apartments with kitchenettes are especially good and there's an outdoor hot tub with mountain views. There is a golf course and swimming pool nearby, and regular shuttle buses into town.

Viking Village
MAP P6 ■ Strandgata 55, 220 Hafnarfjörður ■ 565 1213 ■ www.fjorukrain.is ■ Ⓚ
A whole complex built around a Viking theme, with accommodation, restaurants and Viking entertainment. The exterior of the hotel has a slight warehouse feel, but the rooms are surprisingly good. There are also 14 Viking-themed cottages near the hotel.

Rejkjavík City Hostel
MAP R3 ■ Sundlaugarvegur 34, 105 Reykjavík ■ 553 8110 ■ www.hostel.is ■ Ⓚ
One of the few Icelandic HI Hostels with private rooms as well as dormitories, which, along with its location near the Botanic Gardens and Laugardalur swimming pool, makes it the best budget option in town. Booking in advance is recommended.

22 Hill Hotel
MAP N3 ■ Brautarholt 22–24, 105 Reykjavík ■ 511 3777 ■ 22hillhotel.is ■ ⓀⓀ
A drab exterior but the decent-sized rooms with views, friendly staff, good restaurant and location make this option a firm favourite among visitors.

Hótel Örkin
MAP P4 ■ Brautarholt 29, 105 Reykjavík ■ 568 0777 ■ www.hotelorkin.is ■ ⓀⓀ
Small budget hotel run by the Faroese Seamen's Mission. It is well cared for and has a friendly atmosphere. The room prices include breakfast and freshly baked cakes in the afternoon.

Hótel Ísland
MAP R4 ■ Ármúli 9, 108 Reykjavík ■ 595 7000 ■ www.hotelisland.is ■ ⓀⓀ
Large hotel with colourful furnishings, breaking away from the spartan palettes usually associated with Icelandic accommodation. Bonuses include its location (close to the Botanic Gardens) and free access to the swimming pools of Reykjavík. The Café Island restaurant only serves dinner in the summer.

Grand Hótel Reykjavík
MAP Q3 ■ Sigtún 38, 105 Reykjavík ■ 514 8000 ■ www.grand.is ■ ⓀⓀⓀ
Iceland's largest hotel is situated in an impressive tower block. It has a modern restaurant and a huge spa and fitness centre. The conference rooms make it an ideal business venue.

Hilton Reykjavík Nordica
MAP Q4 ■ Suðurlandsbraut 2, 108 Reykjavík ■ 444 5000 ■ www.hiltonreykjavik.com ■ ⓀⓀⓀ
As the name suggests, the decor here is distinctly biased towards mono-chromatic furnishings and pine flooring. The in-room safes and blackout curtains (for the luminous summer nights) are a nice touch.

Radisson Blu Saga Hótel
MAP J3 ■ Hagatorg, 107 Reykjavík ■ 525 9900 ■ www.radissonblu.com ■ ⓀⓀⓀ
Located close to the city centre, this business and conference venue enjoys lovely views over Reykjavík. The master suite is very stylish, with dark wooden floors and a private balcony. All guests have access to the luxurious hotel spa and health centre.

Hotels Around Iceland

Fosshotel Skaftafell
MAP F5 ▪ Freysnes, 785 Öræfi ▪ 478 1945 ▪ www. hotelskaftafell.is ▪ ⓀⓀ
The amazing glacier views are unfortunately, only visible from a few of the rooms. Otherwise a perfectly comfortable base for hiking at nearby Skaftafell National Park.

Hótel Búðir
MAP A4 ▪ Hótel Búðir, 365 Snæfellsnes ▪ 435 6700 ▪ www.budir.is ▪ ⓀⓀ
This elegantly refurbished old-style hotel is one of Iceland's romantic gems. It has an atmospheric seaside setting, with only a dark wooden church and the nearby white cone of Snæfellsjökull for company. The restaurant is renowned for it's fresh fish and lamb dishes.

Hótel Framtíð
MAP G4 ▪ Vogaland 4, 765 Djúpivogur ▪ 478 8887 ▪ www.hotel framtid.com ▪ ⓀⓀ
This delightful old building overlooks the attractive village harbour of Djúpivogur and is a good place to rest after a trip to Papey island. There are modern rooms in the main hotel and ordinary wooden cabins for hire and a nearby camp site.

Hótel Gígur
MAP F2 ▪ Skútustaðir, 600 Mývatn ▪ 464 4455 ▪ www.keahotels.is ▪ ⓀⓀ
This well managed, modern hotel on the southern shore of Mývatn has amazing views out over the lake from the dining room. The rooms are all recently renovated.

Watch out for the flies outside the lobby during the summer. Free Wi-Fi in every room.

Hótel Ísafjörður
MAP B2 ▪ Silfurtorg 2, 400 Ísafjörður ▪ 456 4111 ▪ www.hotelisafjordur.is ▪ ⓀⓀ
The solid exterior, providing protection against the severe winter storms, hides a warm, comfortable and friendly hotel. The staff go out of their way to be helpful. The rooms are not huge, but have everything you will need for a night or two. The restaurant is decent, if slightly on the expensive side.

Hótel KEA
MAP E2 ▪ Hafnarstræti 87–89, 600 Akureyri ▪ 460 2000 ▪ www. keahotels.is ▪ ⓀⓀ
Located in a grand old building in the heart of Akureyri, this is the flagship hotel in north Iceland of the small KEA chain. The rooms are well furnished and quite spacious. There is a bistro and bar, and the generous buffet breakfast is the ideal start to the day.

Icelandair Hótel Hamar
MAP B4 ▪ Golfvöllurinn Hamar, 310 Borgarnes ▪ 433 6600 ▪ www.iceland airhotels.com ▪ ⓀⓀ
This long, low hotel in a peaceful setting comes complete with outdoor hot tubs, a top-notch restaurant and an excellent 18-hole golf course. There are great mountain views and each room has a large window and a door opening directly onto the grounds.

Do not miss out on a visit to the Borgarnes Settlement Centre during your stay here.

Icelandair Hótel Hérað
MAP G3 ▪ Miðvangur 5-7, 700 Egilsstaðir ▪ 471 1500 ▪ www.iceland hotels.com ▪ ⓀⓀ
The exterior should not deter you. The large rooms are tastefully furnished and another bonus is the helpful staff. The restaurant is fine but Café Nielsen (open summer only), up the road in the oldest house in town, is better value.

Icelandair Hótel Klaustur
MAP E5 ▪ Klausturvegur 6, 880 Kirkjubæjarklaustur ▪ 444 4000 ▪ www.iceland airhotels.com ▪ ⓀⓀ
It may seem strange to find such a large hotel in such a tiny place, but it is well placed for summer excursions to Skaftafell National Park and the Lakagígar craters. There is a decent restaurant and a bar with an outdoor terrace, as well as a small geothermal pool next door.

Leirubakki
MAP D5 ▪ Leirubakki ▪ 487 8700 ▪ www. leirubakki.is ▪ ⓀⓀ
What makes this comfortable, blandly modern hotel exceptional is its location in the heart of south Iceland and within sight of the smouldering ridge of Hekla, one of Iceland's most active volcanoes. Guests can enjoy the outdoor natural thermal spring built of lava blocks with beautiful views.

Hótel Rangá
MAP C5 ▪ Hótel Rangá, Ringroad, near Hella ▪ 487 5700 ▪ www. hotelranga.is ▪ ⓀⓀⓀ
Countryside retreat with 4-star comforts, especially worthwhile if salmon fishing on the nearby Rangá river. The lodge-style pine cabins and main buildings are perfectly decorated and there is an excellent restaurant. Close to all of south Iceland's best attractions.

Guesthouses

Gistiheimilið Baldursbrá
MAP L4 ▪ Laufásvegur 41, 101 Reykjavík ▪ 552 6646 ▪ notendur.centrum.is/ heijfis ▪ Ⓚ
In a residential area close to the bus terminal, this family-run place provides spacious rooms with shared bathrooms and an outdoor hot tub.

Gistiheimilið Geysir
MAP C5 ▪ Geysir ▪ 486 87 33 ▪ www.geysirgolf.is ▪ Ⓚ
Next to the geothermal springs area, this self-catering guesthouse has single, double and triple rooms with a large kitchen. Most suited to groups, but can accommodate individual guests. Book in advance.

Gistiheimilið Hamar
MAP C6 ▪ Herjólfsgata 4, Heimaey, Vestmannaeyjar ▪ 481 2900 ▪ Open May–Sep ▪ www.hotelvestma nnaeyjar.is ▪ Ⓚ
Seasonal budget wing of Hótel Þórshamar, which also runs another guesthouse and a youth hostel. This modern block near the harbour has

comfortable rooms. Breakfast is available in the main hotel.

Gistiheimilið Sunna
MAP M3 ▪ Þórsgata 26, 101 Reykjavík ▪ 511 5570 ▪ www.sunna.is ▪ Ⓚ
Close to Hallgrímskirkja, rooms are clean with access to a kitchenette, and shared or private bathrooms. A buffet breakfast is included. Noise can be a problem in the late-partying city.

Lava Hostel
MAP B5 ▪ Hjallabraut 51, 220 Hafnarfjörður ▪ 565 0900 ▪ www.lavahostel.is ▪ Ⓚ
This simple, self-catering guesthouse has 2 to 6 beds per room, shared bathrooms and full kitchen facilities. There is also a dormitory with sleeping-bag accommodation (bring your own or rent linen here). Buses to Reykjavík and the international airport stop nearby.

Skálholtsskóli
MAP C5 ▪ Skálholt ▪ 486 8870 ▪ www.skalholt.is ▪ Ⓚ
The accommodation is attached to the cathedral school at the historic site of Skálholt. Summer concerts at the cathedral are a bonus (www. sumartonleikar.is) – with contemporary religious music and early music. Book in advance.

Sólheimar Eco-Village
MAP C5 ▪ Grímsnes, 801 Selfoss ▪ 480 4483 ▪ www.solheimar.is ▪ Ⓚ
A stay in this world renowned sustainable community, founded in

1930, is an unforgettable experience. As well as the comfortable guesthouse with access to a swimming pool and hot tub, there are crafts workshops, a café and a sculpture garden.

Welcome Hotel in Vik
MAP D6 ▪ Vikurbraut 26, Vík ▪ 487 1212 ▪ www. vikhotel.is ▪ ⓀⓀ
This charming, guesthouse-like hotel is nestled below seabird-infested slopes and within a short walk of Vík's famous rock formations and black-sand beach. Hotel rooms are int the more modern main wing, with self-catering budget facilities in a separate tin-sided building.

Gistihúsið Egilsstöðum
MAP G3 ▪ Egilsstaðir ▪ 471 1114 ▪ www.lakehotel.is ▪ ⓀⓀ
With a cozy family-run atmosphere this comfortable hotel is set in a large renovated farmhouse just outside of town and with great views over the lake. Rooms are all en suite. There is a great restaurant and it's a perfect base to explore all East Iceland has to offer.

Gistiheimilið Hof
MAP A4 ▪ Hofgarðar, 365 Snæfellsbær ▪ 846 3897 ▪ www.gistihof.is ▪ ⓀⓀ
Long, turf-roofed building in a panoramic rural location near to a sandy beach The guesthouse has six self-contained units, with three double bedrooms, a bathroom, kitchenette and outdoor hot tub. There are 14 en suite rooms available in the summer.

For a key to hotel price categories see p128

Guesthouse Anna

MAP L4 ■ Smáragötu 16,
101 Reykjavík ■ 562 1618
■ www.guesthouseanna.
is ■ Ⓚ Ⓚ
The rooms in this
beautiful and comfortable
house a few minutes walk
from central Reykjavik are
large and have either en
suite or come with shared
bathrooms. With fantastic
food and an extremely
welcoming host, the
house is also well located
in a quiet street close to
the bus station.

Summer Hotels and Eddas

Hólar í Hjaltadal

MAP D2 ■ Hólar, near
Sauðárkrókur ■ 849 6348
■ Open Jun–Aug ■ www.
holar.is/en ■ Ⓚ
The small community of
Hólar is home to a
historically important
cathedral, the island's
largest estate and Hólar
University, where student
accommodation is
available to tourists.

Hótel Edda Höfn

MAP G5 ■ Höfn ■ 444
4850 ■ Open May–Sep ■
www.hoteledda.is ■ Ⓚ
Well placed for glacier
trips to Vatnajökull or
hiking in the Lónsöræfi
reserve, these school
buildings offer
straightforward double
rooms and dormitories
with shared bathrooms
and toilets, plus a
restaurant that is well
known for its delicious
evening buffets.

Hótel Edda Skógar

MAP D6 ■ Skógar ■ 444
4830 ■ Open Jun–Aug ■
www.hoteledda.is ■ Ⓚ
Storm-proof building
neighbouring one of
Iceland's most impressive
waterfalls, Skogafoss,
the eccentric Skógar
Museum and the superb
hiking trail to Þórsmörk.
Plain, serviceable rooms
with shared bathroom
facilities, sleeping-bag
space and a restaurant
serving a plentiful
breakfast buffet and a la
carte dinner are available.

Hótel Edda Stórutjarnir

MAP E2 ■ Stórutjarnir,
Route 1 ■ 444 4890 ■
Open Jun–Aug ■ www.
hoteledda.is ■ Ⓚ
Conveniently located
between Akureyri and
Mývatn, this modern
lakeside hotel sits in a
short, tight valley
frequented by geese in
the summer. Rooms
include private en suite
doubles as well as
dormitories. There is also
a restaurant and an
attached thermal pool.

Hótel Edda Vík

MAP D6 ■ Route 1, Vík í
Mýrdal ■ 444 4840 ■
Open May–Sep ■ www.
hoteledda.is ■ Ⓚ
This Edda hotel is classier
than most, with en suite
double rooms in the main
building and self-
contained wooden cabins
on the grassy slopes at
the rear. Breakfast is
served in the lobby; head
to Vík for other meals.

Hótel Hallormstaður

MAP G3 ■ Hallormstaður,
near Egilsstaðir ■ 471
2400 ■ www.hotel701.is ■
Ⓚ
Cozy country hotel inside
Iceland's most extensive
forest, close to Lögurinn
lake. The hotel has self-
contained wooden
cottages, rooms in a large

guesthouse and summer-
only accommodation.
Guests can choose from
two hotel restaurants.

Fosshótel Vatnajökull

MAP G5 ■ Route 1 near
Höfn, Hornafjörður ■ 478
2555 ■ www.fosshotel.is
■ Ⓚ Ⓚ
This is a functional, tidy
place, with warm but
small and simply
furnished rooms that
have breakfast included in
the price. Given the
location, you should pay
extra to get a room with
glacier views. This is a
popular stopover for large
tour groups.

Hótel Aldan

MAP H3 ■ Norðurgata 2,
710 Seyðisfjörður ■ 472
1277 ■ www.hotelaldan.
is ■ Ⓚ Ⓚ
A 19th-century wooden
building by the harbour,
once a bank, has been
converted into this nine-
bedroom hotel, which
retains a historic
atmosphere with period
furnishings. There is a bar
and an excellent
restaurant. More rooms
are available in the nearby
sister operation, Hótel
Snæfell, which is run by
the same family.

Hótel Edda Ísafjörður

MAP B2 ■ Torfnes,
Ísafjörður ■ 444 4960 ■
Open Jun–Aug ■ www.
hoteledda.is ■ Ⓚ Ⓚ
Located near the centre
of Ísafjörður, this school
(for most of the year) has
good facilities. Rooms
have en suite bathrooms
or in-room washbasins.
There is a camp
site and sleeping-bag
space in the heated
sports hall. Buffet
breakfast is available.

Hótel Edda ML Laugarvatn
MAP C5 ■ Laugarvatn ■ 444 4810 ■ Open Jun–Aug ■ www.hoteledda.is ■ ⓚⓚ

One of two Eddas in town, this huge complex offers double rooms that are either en suite or have shared bathrooms. There is an in-house restaurant and it is close to the Golden Circle attractions, a huge pool and Laugarvatn lake.

Camp Sites and Character Stays

Egilsstaðir Campsite
MAP G3 ■ Kaupvangur 17, 700 Egilsstaðir ■ 470 0750 ■ www.east.is ■ ⓚ

Scruffy and occasionally boggy camping ground with some sheltered woody patches near Egilsstaðir's tourist information and long-distance bus stop; you need to choose your site carefully. Good shower and toilet facilities and a tiny, sheltered barbecue and seating area.

Galtalækur II
MAP C5 ■ Route 26, Rangárþing ytra, Hella ■ 487 6528 ■ www.1.is/gl2/en ■ ⓚ

Camp site and self-contained cabins near Hekla volcano, Tangavatn lake and Þjófafoss waterfall. You can buy fishing licences here.

Hamrar Campsite
MAP E2 ■ Kjarnaskógur, Akureyri ■ 461 2264 ■ www.hamrar.is ■ ⓚ

Enormous camping grounds near woodland outside Akureyri in the north of the island. You do not need to reserve a space in advance. There are toilets, hot showers, washing machines and tumble dryers on site, along with a kitchen and a covered dining area.

Hlíð Campsite
MAP F2 ■ Reykjahlíð, Mývatn ■ 464 4103 ■ www.hlidmyv.is ■ ⓚ

This is a great place to base yourself while at Mývatn; there are superb views over Reykjahlíð and the lake. The site offers hot showers, toilets and outdoor sinks for washing laundry or plates and cutlery. Wooden cabins and a dorm building are available for those who arrive without a tent.

Reykjavík Campsite
MAP R2 ■ Sundlaugarvegur 34, 104 Reykjavík ■ 568 6944 ■ www.reykjavikcampsite.is ■ ⓚ

The huge grassy slope of this camp site has room for hundreds of tents. A 20-minute walk from the city centre, the site has a covered cooking area, washing machine, tumble dryer, toilets and showers.

Hótel Dyrhólaey
MAP D6 ■ Near Vík ■ 487 1333 ■ www.dyrholaey.is ■ ⓚ

This lakeside farmstead is nestled in the hills above Dyrhólaey bird reserve. The fully equipped rooms come complete with private bathrooms and are clean, warm and very comfortable. North facing rooms have good views of the Mýrdalsjökull icecap. Staff are helpful and the restaurant offers a healthy breakfast and good-value evening buffet of Icelandic dishes.

Hótel Anna
MAP D6 ■ Moldnúpur, Route 246, between Skógar and Seljarlandsfoss ■ 487 8950 ■ www.hotelanna.is ■ ⓚⓚⓚ

Red-roofed farmhouse in a great rural location with Eyjafjallajökull rising above it. Large beds, low ceilings and old wooden furniture add to the character. Price includes buffet breakfast and use of hot tubs and sauna.

Hótel Laki
MAP E5 ■ Efri Vík, Kirkjubæjarklaustur ■ 412 4600 ■ www.hotellaki.is ■ ⓚⓚⓚ

Converted farmhouse with en suite doubles in the main building and self-contained cabins suitable for groups alongside it. Located on the edge of a pseudo-crater and a lava field stretching to Lakagígar.

Hótel Látrabjarg
MAP A2 ■ Near Route 612/615 junction, Patreksfjörður ■ 456 1500 ■ Open mid-May–Sep ■ www.latrabjarg.com ■ ⓚⓚⓚ

Originally a boarding school, this hotel is close to the beach and bird cliffs. Rooms have en suite or shared bathrooms. Freshwater trout fishing and horse riding available.

Hótel Tindastóll
MAP D2 ■ Lindargata 3, Sauðárkrókur ■ 453 5002 ■ www.hoteltindastoll.com ■ ⓚⓚⓚ

Iceland's oldest hotel opened in 1884 and has an outdoor spa. Rooms have a warm and cozy feel. A resident ghost adds to the atmosphere.

For a key to hotel price categories see p128

General Index

Acknowledgments

Author

David Leffman is a travel writer and photographer who first visited Iceland in 1981. Apart from *Top 10 Iceland*, he has authored *Eyewitness China* for DK, along with guidebooks to Iceland, Australia, Indonesia, China and Hong Kong for Rough Guides. He has also led specialist guided tours to China.

Contents Outline
Michael Kissane

Publishing Director Georgina Dee

Publisher Vivien Antwi

Design Director Phil Ormerod

Editorial Emma Brady, Michelle Crane, Rachel Fox, Freddie Marriage, Fíodhna Ní Ghríofa, Sally Schafer, Neil Simpson, Christine Stroyan

Design Richard Czapnik, Sunita Gahir

Picture Research Phoebe Lowndes, Susie Peachey, Ellen Root, Oran Tarjan

Cartography Stuart James, Zafar-ul-Islam Khan, Suresh Kumar, Casper Morris

DTP Jason Little, George Nimmo

Production Nancy-Jane Maun

Factchecker Paul Sullivan

Proofreader Kate Berens

Indexer Helen Peters

Phrase Book Bergljót Njóla Jakobsdóttir

Commissioned Photography Nigel Hicks, Rough Guides/David Leffman

Picture Credits

The publisher would like to thank the following for their kind permission to reproduce their photographs:
(**Key:** a-above; b-below/bottom; c-centre; f-far; l-left; r-right; t-top)

4Corners: SIME/Olimpio Fantuz 3tl, 72-3; SIM /Maurizio Rellini 56-7.

Alamy Images: Arctic Images 70tl, 70bc; Icelandic photo agency 67br;Mary Evans Picture Library 36tl; Graham Prentice 74tl; Steven Sheppardson 37bl; Clive Tully 20cla.

Austur Club : Thorgeir Olafsson 66cla.

Corbis: Arctic-Images/SuperStock 50t; Arctic-Images 4b, 55tr, 58br, 116b; Hans Strand 115t.

Dreamstime.com: Sylvia Adams 32clb; Adreslebedev 4clb; Aiisha 4t; Aivolie 68crb; Steve Allen 22-3; Andreanita 24bl; Claudio Balducelli 20-1c; Gisli Baldursson 33tl, 53tr; Darius Baužys 13tl; Andrey Bayda 49tl; Bilderschorsch 104bl; Sigurdur William Brynjarsson 2tr, 34-5; Tomáš Bureš 47bc; Cadifor 103bc; Checco 52br, 60t; Chrishowey 51br; Demerzel21 2tl, 8-9, 105-6,;Derwuth 76b; Dieniti 4crb; Filip Fuxa 1, 7cr, 10bl, 46crb, 85bl; Gkoultouridis 16-7c; H368k742 55clb, 69tr; Jon Helgason 46tc; Humgate 7tr, Iaceo 6cl, Martín Zalba Ibanez 32br, 68t, Jarcosa98crb; Javarman 30-1c; Jeremyreds 3tr, 118-9; Aagje De Jong 61cl; Þórarinn Jónsson 45b; Thomas Langlands 27tl, Mihai-bogdan Lazar 14-5c; Florence Mcginn 28-9c, minnystock 11t, Erzsi Molnár 53cl; Anna Pakutina 21tl; Parys 48bl; Pedja77 52clb; Johann Ragnarsson 49crb; Michael Ransburg 18-9c, 51tl; Arseniy Rogov 48tc; Sanspek 4cla; Serinus 4cl; Rafn Sigurbjörnsson 11crb; Marteinn Sigurdsson 90cra; Leonid Spektor 103tl; Kippy Spilker 13cr; Alexey Stiop 29cl; Tatonka 96b; Ryan Taylor 10-1b; Milan_tesar 31bl; Tomas1111 26cl, 39tl; Topdeq 24cl; Ucheema 4cra; Ukrphoto 63tr; Victorianl 11cra; Corepics Vof 30bl; Wkruck 11c; Zbindere 89br.

Einar Jonsson Sculpture Museum: 40crb.

Fishmarkadurinn: Bjorn Arnason 63cl.

FLPA: Bill Coster 20b; ImageBroker 69br.

Getty Images: Patrick Dieudonne 86tc; Michele Falzone 42tr; Atli Mar Hafsteinsson 86bl; Thorsten Henn 59cl; Lonely Planet Images 6tr; Richard Manin 42bl; Martin Moos 88tl.

Hamborgarabúllan: 64b.

Inside the Volcano: Sølve Fredheim 112bl.

Kirsuberjatréð: 79tr.

Micro Bar: 66tr.

Photoshot: Stefan Auth 94tl; Picture Alliance/Carsten Schmidt 24br.

Prikið Kaffhús: 66br.

Rauða Húsið: 113tr.

Rex Features: Agencia EFE 71tr.

Reykjavik City Museum: G. Bjarki Gudmundsson 41bl.

Sigurjón Ólafsson Museum: Embrace - NATO, 1949, by Sigurjón Ólafsson LSÓ 1102 41tr.

Við Tjörnina: 81tl.

Þrír Frakkar: Picasa 65cr.

Jacket

Front and spine – **Getty Images**: Chris Hepburn, b L. Toshio Kishiyama t.

Back – **Alamy Images**: PhotoAlto/ Sandro Di Carlo Darsa t.

Pull out map cover

Getty Images: Chris Hepburn b, L. Toshio Kishiyama t.

All other images © Dorling Kindersley For further information see: www. dkimages.com

*As a guide to abbreviations in visitor information blocks: **Adm** = admission charge.*

Penguin Random House

Printed and bound in China

First published in Great Britain in 2010 by Dorling Kindersley Limited 80 Strand, London WC2R 0RL

Copyright 2010, 2016 © Dorling Kindersley Limited

A Penguin Random House Company

15 16 17 18 10 9 8 7 6 5 4 3 2

Reprinted with revisions 2012, 2014, 2016

A CIP catalogue record is available from the British Library.

ISBN 978 0 2411 9854 4

MIX
Paper from responsible sources
FSC™ C018179
www.fsc.org

SPECIAL EDITIONS OF DK TRAVEL GUIDES

DK Travel Guides can be purchased in bulk quantities at discounted prices for use in promotions or as premiums. We are also able to offer special editions and personalized jackets, corporate imprints, and excerpts from all of our books, tailored specifically to meet your own needs.

To find out more, please contact:

in the US
specialsales@dk.com

in the UK
travelguides@uk.dk.com

in Canada
specialmarkets@dk.com

in Australia
penguincorporatesales@ penguinrandomhouse.com.au

Phrase Book

Icelandic is a Nordic language. Many of its sounds do not exist in English, so the pronunciations below are for guidance only. Icelandic has three letters that do not exist in modern English: þ ("thorn", pronounced as th as in "thin"); ð ("eth", pronounced as soft th as in "the"); æ ("aye", pronounced as i as in "light"). Stress falls on the first syllable of the word.

Guidelines for Pronunciation
Vowels
There are seven vowels – a, e, i, o, u, y and æ, five of which take a stress accent, which changes the pronunciation. The "o" can have an umlaut over it.

a = as in "sat"	*á* = ow as in "owl"
e = as in "met"	*i* = as in "sit"
í = ee as in "feel"	*o* = as in "hot"
ó = as in "hole"	*ö* = "uh" sound
u = as in "put"	*ú* = oo as in "fool"
ý = ee as in "meet"	*æ* = i as in "light"

Letter combinations
Some combined letters in Icelandic have special pronunciations.

au = as o in "hole"	*ei* = as ai in "hail"
ey = as ai in "hail"	*fn* = as bn
ll = as tl	*sj* = as sh in "fish"
fl = as bl, but as fl at the start of a word	
ng = as nk at the end of a word, as ng in the middle	

In an Emergency

Help!	**Hjálp!**	*hy-oulp*
Call a doctor	**Náið í lækni**	*nou-ith ee laek-ni*
Call an ambulance	**Hringdu í sjúkrabíl**	*hreen-du ee syoo-kra-beel*
Call the police	**Hringdu í lögregluna**	*hreen-du ee leu-rekl-una*
Call the fire brigade	**Hringdu í slökkviliðið**	*hreen-du ee sleuk-vi-lith-ith*

Communication Essentials

Yes	**Já**	*yow*
No	**Nei**	*nay*
Please (offering)	**Gjörðu svo vel**	*gyeurth-u svo vel*
Thank you	**Takk/takk fyrir**	*takk /takk fir-ir*
Excuse me	**Afsakið**	*af-sak-ith*
Hello	**Halló**	*hallo*
Hello (polite)	**Vertu sæl/sæll**	*vert-u sael(f.)/saetl(m.)*
Goodbye	**Bless**	*bless*
Good night /morning /evening	**Góða nótt /morgunn Gott kvöld**	*go-tha nott go-tha morg-un gott kveu-ld*

Useful Phrases

How are you?	**Hvað segirðu gott?**	*kvahth say-irth-u gott*
Very well, thank you.	**Allt gott**	*alht gott*
That's fine.	**Það er fínt/ gott**	*thath er feen-t/ gott*
Where is/ are …?	**Hvar er/ eru …?**	*kvar er/ eru*
How do I get to …?	**Hvernig kemst ég til …?**	*kvern-ig kem-st yieg til*

Do you speak English?	**Talarðu ensku?**	*tal-arth-u ensk-u*
I don't understand.	**Ég skil ekki**	*yieg skil ekki*

Shopping

How much does this cost?	**Hvað kostar þetta?**	*kvath kost-ar thett-a*
I would like …	**Ég ætla að fá …**	*yieg aetla ath fou*
Do you take … credit cards? traveller's cheques?	**Takið þið … kreditkort? ferðatékka?**	*tak-ith thith kre-dit-kort ferth-a-tiekk-a*
What time do you open/ close?	**Hvenær opnið þið/ lokið þið?**	*kven-aer oph-nith thith/ lok-ith thith?*
this one	**þessi hérna**	*thessi hier-nah*
that one	**þessi þarna**	*thessi thar-nah*
expensive	**dýrt**	*deer-t*
size	**stærð**	*sdaerth*

Types of Shop

bakery	**bakarí**	*ba-ka-ree*
bank	**banki**	*boun-ki*
chemist	**apótek**	*ap-o-tek*
fishmonger	**fiskibúð**	*fisk-i-booth*
garage (mechanics)	**bílaverkstæði**	*beel-a-verk-staeth-i*
market	**markaður**	*mark-ath-ur*
post office	**pósthús**	*post-hoos*
supermarket	**matarverslun**	*mah-dar-vers-lun*
travel agent	**ferðaskrifstofa**	*fertha-skrif-sdofa*

Sightseeing

art gallery	**listagallerí**	*list-ah-gall-er-ee*
bay	**flói**	*flo-i*
beach	**fjara**	*fyar-ah*
bike	**reiðhjól**	*raith-hyeeol*
bus (town)	**strætó**	*straeh-tou*
bus (long dist.)	**rúta**	*roo-ta*
bus station	**umferðamiðstöð**	*um-fertha-mithsteuth*
bus ticket	**strætó/rútu miði**	*straeh-tou/roo-tu mithi*
car	**bíll**	*bee-dlh*
car rental	**bílaleiga**	*bee-la-laig-a*
cathedral	**dómkirkja**	*dom-kirk-ya*
church	**kirkja**	*kirk-ya*
glacier	**jökull**	*yeu-kudl*
harbour	**höfn**	*heubn*
hot spring	**hver**	*kver*
island	**eyja**	*ai-yah*
lake	**stöðuvatn**	*steu-thu-vatn*
mountain	**fjall**	*fyadlh*
museum	**safn**	*sabn*
tourist information	**upplýsingamiðstöð**	*uph-lees-eengamith-sdeuth*
waterfall	**foss**	*foss*

Staying in a Hotel

Do you have a vacant room?	**Eigið þið laust herbergi?**	*aigith thith laost her-berg-i*
double room with double bed	**Tveggja manna herbergi með hjónarúmi**	*tvegg-ya mann-a her-berg-i meth hyonah-roommi*
twin room	**tveggja manna herbergi**	*tvegg-ya mann-a her-berg-i*

single room	eins manns herbergi	*ayns manns her-berg-i*
room with bath/shower	herbergi með baði/sturtu	*her-berg-i meth bath-i/sturh-ta*
I have a reservation	Ég á pantað	*yieg ou pant-ath*

Eating Out

Have you got a table?	Eigið þið laust borð?	*aigith thith laost borth*
I'd like to reserve a table.	Gæti ég pantað borð.	*gyaet-i yieg pant-ath borth*
breakfast	morgunmatur	*morg-un-mat-ur*
lunch	hádegismatur	*hou-deg-is-mat-ur*
dinner	kvöldmatur	*kveuld-mat-ur*
The bill, please.	Reikninginn takk.	*raikn-ing-inn takk*
waitress/waiter	þjónn	*thyo-dn*
menu	matseðill	*maht-seth-idl*
starter	smáréttur	*smou-riet-ur*
first course	forréttur	*for-riet-ur*
main course	aðalréttur	*athal-riet-ur*
dessert	eftirréttur	*eft-ir-riet-ur*
wine list	vínlisti	*veen-list-i*
glass	glas	*glas*
bottle	flaska	*flask-a*
knife	hnífur	*hneev-ur*
fork	gaffall	*gaff-adl*
spoon	skeið	*skaith*

Menu Decoder

bjór	*byorh*	beer
brauð	*braoth*	bread
ferskir ávextir	*fersk-ir ou-vekst-irh*	fresh fruit
fiskur	*fisk-ur*	fish
franskar	*fransk-ar*	chips
grænmeti	*graen-met-i*	vegetables
grillað	*grill-ath*	grilled
gufusoðið	*gu-vu-soth-ith*	poached
hvítvín	*kveet-veen*	white wine
ís	*ees*	ice cream
kaka/ vínarbrauð	*ca-ka/ veen-ar-braoth*	cake/ pastry
kartöflur	*kart-eufl-ur*	potatoes
kjöt	*kyeut*	meat
kjúklingur	*kyook-leeng-ur*	chicken
lambakjöt	*lamb-ah-kyeut*	lamb
laukur	*laok-ur*	onions
lax	*laks*	salmon
mjólk	*myolk*	milk
nautasteik	*nao-ta-staik*	beef
ostur	*os-tur*	cheese
pipar	*phi-par*	pepper
pylsa/ pulsa	*pils-ah/ pul-sah*	hotdog
rauðvín	*raoth-veen*	red wine
rækjur	*rai-kyur*	prawns
sjávarréttur	*syou-va-rietd-ur*	seafood
smjör	*smyeurh*	butter
soðið	*soth-ith*	boiled
sódavatn	*so-da-vadn*	mineral water
sósa	*so-sa*	sauce
steikt	*staikt*	fried
súkkulaði	*sook-u-lath-i*	chocolate
súpa	*soo-ba*	soup
svínakjöt	*sveen-a-kyeut*	pork

sykur	*siik-ur*	sugar
te	*teh*	tea
vatn	*vahdn*	water
ýsa	*ee-sa*	haddock

Useful Signs

open	opið	*op-ith*
closed	lokað	*lohk-ath*
entry	inn/inngangur	*inn/inn-goung-ur*
exit	út/útgangur	*oot/oot-goung-ur*
jeep track	jeppaslóð	*yepp-ah-sloth*
parking	bílastæði	*bee-la-staeth-i*
one-lane bridge	einbreið brú	*ayn-braith broo*
danger	hætta	*haett-ah*
forbidden	bannað	*bann-ath*
end of tarmac	malbik slitlag endar	*mal-bik slit-lag end-ar*
campsite	tjaldsvæði	*tyald-svaethi*
toilet	klósett	*clo-sett*
ladies' toilet	kvennaklósett	*kvenn-a-clo-sett*
gents' toilet	karlaklósett	*karl-a-clo-sett*

Time

one minute	ein mínúta	*ayn meen-oot-a*
one hour	ein klukkustund	*ayn kluk-u-stun-dh*
a day	dagur	*dag-ur*
Monday	mánudagur	*moun-u-dag-ur*
Tuesday	þriðjudagur	*thrith-yu-dag-ur*
Wednesday	miðvikudagur	*mith-vik-u-dag-ur*
Thursday	fimmtudagur	*fimt-u-dag-ur*
Friday	föstudagur	*feust-u-dag-ur*
Saturday	laugardagur	*laog-ar-dag-ur*
Sunday	sunnudagur	*sunnu-dag-ur*

Numbers

1	einn	*aydn*
2	tveir	*tvayr*
3	þrír	*threer*
4	fjórir	*fyor-ir*
5	fimm	*fim*
6	sex	*segs*
7	sjö	*syeu*
8	átta	*outt-a*
9	níu	*nee-u*
10	tíu	*tee-u*
11	ellefu	*edl-ev-u*
12	tólf	*tolvh*
13	þrettán	*thrett-dyoun*
14	fjórtán	*fyorh-dyoun*
15	fimmtán	*fim-dyoun*
16	sextán	*segs-dyoun*
17	sautján	*sao-dyoun*
18	átján	*out-dyoun*
19	nítján	*nee-dyoun*
20	tuttugu	*tutt-ug-u*
21	tuttugu og einn	*tutt-ug-u og aydn*
30	þrjátíu	*thryou-tee-u*
40	fjörtíu	*fyeur-tee-u*
50	fimmtíu	*fim-tee-u*
60	sextíu	*segs-tee-u*
70	sjötíu	*syeu-tee-u*
80	áttatíu	*outt-a-tee-u*
90	níutíu	*nee-u-tee-u*
100	hundrað	*hund-rath*
1000	þúsund	*thoos-und*
1,000,000	milljón	*mil-ee-yon*

Iceland Town Index

Reykjavík Selected Street Index